AMAZING
ASHVILLE

Brooke,

Congratulations on your achievement!
May you always cherish your time at
Teays Valley and know that no matter
where you go or whatever you do in life,
you will always belong to this fascinating
community!

— Bob Hei...

Library of Congress Control Number: 2019952610

ISBN: 9781681062525

Illustrations by Bob Hines.

Printed in the United States of America
20 21 22 23 24   5 4 3 2 1

The Most Colorful Community in America

AMAZING
ASHVILLE

FEATURING

THE DOG THAT VOTED REPUBLICAN, THE WORLD RECORD TRAFFIC LIGHT, *AND* SHOT DEAD BY A MAD COW

BOB HINES

Dedication

This book is dedicated to all of the residents of the Teays Valley School District, but especially to the founders and core group of people that, against all odds, found a way to create a museum about the wonderful and weird aspects of small-town life—Mona Lee Morrison, Jack Lemon, Charles Cordle, Herman and Kathryn Petty, Marguerite Brokaw, Georgia Dore, Larry and Sue Toole, Bronson Kitchen, Rodger Southward, Iona Hines, Art and Ada Lou Deal, Frank and Madge Baum, Will Fischer, Chet Gloyd, and hundreds of others like Mike and Linda Cummins, Jim-Bob Welsh, Steve Clay, Albert Reinhart, Shirley Marion, Dorothy Cormany, Karl Barch, and John Swingle who have donated their time and resources to help develop Ohio's highly acclaimed Small Town Museum.

All of these people deserve great praise, but there is one person who stands above all the rest—Charles W. Morrison. He really started it all with a small display in his store. His sense of humor and zest for life are the soul of the museum. May it always be so.

Contents

Acknowledgments

A book like this requires a great deal of tenacious research and input from others. Over the years people have come forward with stories and even artifacts associated with those stories. These have been saved and cataloged by people like Charlie Morrison and Dorothy Cormany. Individuals with a passion for uncovering the unusual and a commitment to preserving such artifacts include Tom Zwayer, Brian Meyers, Shoppie Williams, Charles Cordle, Mary Reid, and Mike Cummins.

Volunteer researchers have added contextual information to many of these stories by using the resources at the Ohioana Library, Ohio History Connection, and the Pickaway County Historical & Genealogical Library. I especially want to acknowledge Karl and Angie Finley for their assistance. They provided valuable information related to several of the stories used in this book.

I owe a debt to Gale Leatherwood, Luther Hafey, and Nelle Oesterle of Ashville. Gale compiled a collection of humorous local stories several years ago. The story about Ashville's Sleeping Beauty comes largely from his account. Luther collected material and published his story about George W. Brown in the *Ashville Area Heritage Society Newsletter*. Nelle Oesterle long ago inspired a desire in this author to search for historical accuracy. She also modeled how to use illustrations to complement a narrative when there are no photographs of an event. If you are wondering how she did that, you might want to view her book about George Washington and his travels.

Dr. Chester Rockey was also the original source for stories about John W. Messick and the political rivalry between Tom

Accord and Clyde Brinker. He shared these and other stories in interviews conducted between 1968 and 1975.

Most of the photos are the property of Ohio's Small Town Museum and appear in its collections, but I owe a special thanks to Karl and Angie Finley for the photos of Clyde Michael, the Twin Elms, and the Stage Coach Inn. Jim Mills provided the interior photo of Kaiserman's store, Trish Bennett furnished a photo of the model dress, and Jim Gloyd supplied the photo of *The Wager* movie poster.

It is also important to acknowledge that it is impossible to capture all of the wonderful achievements, local connections to world and national history, and undeniably weird occurrences that are associated with this area. Hopefully the stories that do appear reinforce why this area is definitely America's most colorful community.

Introduction

Ashville and all the other communities in the Teays Valley Local School District are amazing. This area south of Columbus, Ohio, is the most celebrated celebratory rural community in America. Not only do they pull out all the stops for the Fourth of July and the Commercial Point Homecoming, but they also offer a highly regarded Viking Festival, a Karting Classic, and a well-attended Food Truck and Community Festival, all of which help fund local nonprofit activities.

One of the beneficiaries of these celebrations is Ohio's Small Town Museum, which is located in Ashville. National travel writers have called it "one of the best free community museums in America." Unlike many of its contemporaries, it has never sought a single dollar of federal or state support because the museum's officers have always firmly believed in self-reliance and avoided outside assistance. There is a plaque near the entrance of the museum that firmly states this philosophy: "The only thing the government gave us was a hassle."

The sign is there in part because the state made the community remove its beloved traffic light from the main intersection of town—it just did not meet state standards. People would come from all over Ohio just to watch this odd-looking local invention change from green to red and back again. Then the railroad wanted to tear down the town's station or have it burned for firefighting practice. The local newspaper closed its doors, the canning factory folded, and the regional bus line no longer stopped in town.

Economic efficiencies driven by new transportation modes, means of communication, and manufacturing technologies left many rural communities like Ashville behind. In their wake, outside interests began to control nearly all aspects of life—banks, granaries, grocery stores, manufacturing plants, newspapers, and even schools. People in the Ashville area watched this happening in their own community and saw how it was destroying their sense of belonging and pride.

Local residents decided there was one thing that they alone could use to rebuild their sense of pride in community— something of value that belonged to them and nobody else— their past. At the time, they had no idea how rich their local history might be. They just had a belief that there might be hidden local treasure in people's attics, basements, and garages. They were right.

Turns out that their railroad station was the last of the original Scioto Valley Railroad depots, and it was restored by local volunteers. The unusual-looking traffic light now directs traffic at the intersection of weird and wonderful in the museum. It anchors a fabulous collection of local memorabilia from Ashville and the surrounding area that celebrates influential connections to local, national, and world history while at the same time honoring the odd, the strange, and downright weird aspects of communal living.

Amazing Ashville's chapters are organized around the unusual characteristics of the area. Tales about local oddities are aligned with the theme of each chapter. Some might argue that these unfairly characterize rural communities like Ashville as being primarily odd, but the accompanying true side stories depict a broad range of achievements made by current and former residents that should dispel those perceptions. Those wanting to read more about incredible connections and other oddities associated with the amazing Ashville area should check out the Facebook page of Ohio's Small Town Museum or, better yet, come by and give them a visit!

—Bob Hines

The Sycamore Wedding Tree on hole number fifteen at Cook's Creek golf course is massive, but is a baby compared to the World Champion Sycamore that once thrived there.

Chapter One

Natural Wonders

Ohioans affectionately acknowledge a tree that produces poisonous nuts as their state tree and have a state snake (black racer) and insect (ladybug). The state museum has a two-headed calf prominently displayed and the Cleveland Museum of Natural History had Balto—an Alaskan sled dog that saved many lives—immortalized by stuffing his remains.

Ohio's Small Town Museum also pays tribute to a wide variety of flora and fauna. Go there to see a statue of the dog that voted Republican, a stuffed version of the rooster that paid for his own meals, an egg sculpted by a goose, black racer snakes guarding silver nuggets, and displays about unusual trees, flowers, and other natural wonders. Visit to learn about peacock greeters, the original Spider-Man, a gun-toting killer cow, and the chicken that did her part to end the Great Depression.

There are many books about Ohio oddities that acknowledge Ashville's distinct love of natural oddities. In this regard, the Ashville area is unmatched.

The Dog that Voted Republican

Clyde Brinker owned a restaurant in downtown Ashville on Long Street. Two doors down was a barbershop run by Tom Accord. Clyde's restaurant was known as the unofficial Republican headquarters in town and Tom's was the unofficial Democratic headquarters. The two of them had a rather friendly rivalry for decades.

Clyde had a remarkable Boston terrier named Buster that he had trained to do a large number of physical tricks. Buster would jump through Clyde's legs, turn around, and jump on Clyde's back. Part of his repertoire was captured on film.

Well, as the 1928 presidential campaign heated up, Clyde was looking for an edge over his neighbor when he came up with a brilliant idea. He taught Buster to yelp when the name Herbert Hoover was mentioned and to growl menacingly when Al Smith's name was spoken. That was a source of great delight to visitors who came into the restaurant for a bite to eat.

Clyde decided to take Buster down to Tom's to show off the dog's Republican tendencies. Buster gave a masterful performance to all of the patrons waiting for a haircut. Clyde turned to Tom and said, "Tom, as you can see, Buster here is smarter than all of you Democrats." To which Tom retorted, "I am worried that you Republicans are only as smart as your dog."

It's hard to say who got the better of the exchange. Although he is long departed,

Buster with Clyde Brinker

Buster at home on the porch rocker

Buster remains an iconic figure in local lore. The same can be said for Clyde Brinker, who figures prominently in several other stories.

The day pigs flew.

Not sure how Buster would have reacted to this situation, but in 1897 Republicans in the Ohio Senate who had opposed the US Senate appointment of political boss Mark Hanna found themselves in a pickle. Hanna was moving his political forces on the Republican side to consolidate his power in the state. When Hanna was told that a few of his Republican detractors might break ranks and select a Democrat for their senate leader, he said that pigs would fly before that would happen.

According to the *New York Times*, Democratic State Senator Thaddeus Cromley from Ashville was thrust into the national spotlight on January 4, 1898, when a few rogue Republicans in the Ohio Senate teamed up with minority Democrats to make him president pro tem of the Senate. Anti-Hanna Republicans did the unthinkable and elected a Democrat as their leader. Cromley was a farmer and businessman. He was also a proud graduate of Kenyon College. In 1887 and 1889 he was elected to the lower house of the General Assembly of Ohio. In 1890 the Democratic Party nominated him to run for the office of secretary of state. He was defeated, but he was the only Democratic candidate that made a close race of it for state office. He was elected to the state senate in 1895 and reelected in 1897, when he became the floor leader for the Democrats.

Thaddeus E. Cromley

The Rooster that Paid for His Own Meal

Adda Cooper raised an Old English brown-red rooster called "Chic-Chic" as a pet. He would often roost on the back of her front porch rocking chair. There they would greet people passing by.

No one knows exactly when Chic-Chic decided to stroll along the sidewalk down the block to the front of Clyde Brinker's restaurant, which also served as the Lake Shore System bus stop. The Lake Shore was a bus line that ran in this region from Portsmouth to Columbus. Chic-Chic developed a habit of visiting Brinker's precisely when the bus would arrive, and he would welcome the arrivals with a throaty cluck and send them off with the same sound when they would leave. Then Chic-Chic would gather himself and strut back home.

The bus drivers and regular passengers were so amused by his actions that the story made it to folktale author David Webb—whose pen name was "Erasmus Foster Darby." He came to Ashville to meet Mrs. Cooper and chronicled the comings and goings of the famed rooster. It was during this meeting that he learned something else special about this unusual bird.

Mrs. Cooper would place a dime on her porch for Chic-Chic to take to Clyde Brinker's restaurant. She would say, "Chic-

Chic, go to Brinker's for some corn meal," and off he would go with the dime in his beak headed for Clyde's place. When he got there, he pecked on the screen door, and Clyde would exchange a small bowl of meal for the dime.

The debate rages on.

Probably one of the most good-natured debates that continues amongst regulars at the museum centers on who was smarter, Chic-Chic or Buster? Everybody has an opinion, and those who choose one over the other often have complicated reasons for doing so.

You might think that those who are firmly in the Democratic camp would strongly favor Chic-Chic. After all, Buster voted for Herbert Hoover, and Hoover's administration, rightly or wrongly, has been linked to the Great Depression. There are many with a liberal persuasion who do, but some Democrats are quite fond of their dogs and are inclined to believe that dogs are naturally smarter than chickens.

Similarly, there are some more conservative members who believe that Chic-Chic was just naturally inquisitive and had the air of a strongly independent personality. They lean towards believing the Rooster King of Ashville was smarter than Buster because he took the initiative to manage his own kingdom.

No Michelangelo, But . . .

In 1925 farmer Henry Gloyd of Walnut Township had a goose that laid what could only be described as a self-sculptured egg—looking very much like a nesting goose. The egg had a well-defined head, neck, and body.

He was so pleased with his artistic goose's figurine that he brought it to the *Pickaway County News* in Ashville for editor Steve Fridley to look over. Fridley did a story about it on the front page, describing the goose's impressive artistic work.

Fridley ended his story thusly: "Whether the goose was so pleased with the freak egg, or so discouraged, we do not know, but anyway she fixed things up by laying a perfect egg the same day."

The arty egg was placed on display in the window of the *Pickaway County News* office on Wright Street so subscribers could stop by and take a view. Everyone admired the goose's effort but wondered if this was going to be her last foray into the arts. Alas, whatever sparked her creative talents never appeared again, and Henry's hopes of developing the modern equivalent of a golden goose were cooked.

Kermit the frog and the puppetry capital.

The artistic goose was not the only local creative talent carving out a name. There was a time in the late 1950s and early 1960s that the Ashville area could lay claim to the title of puppetry capital of America. The Puppeteers of America was incorporated here and its *Puppetry Journal* was published in Ashville. The Puppeteers of America store was located in South Bloomfield. This was all because educator Vivian Runkle Michael was the editor of the journal and ran the national puppetry store.

Frank Oz and Jim Henson

She and Marjorie Batchelder are also credited with introducing a new style of puppet to America called hand and rod puppets. Jim Henson adapted this idea to make something he called "Muppets." Vivian would be the first to say that Jim Henson took their idea to a different level.

Vivian (Runkle) Michael

She was pleased when Jim accepted the presidency of the Puppeteers of America in 1961. It was at the Puppeteers of America Festival in 1961 that Jim met Jerry Juhl and Frank Oz. They, together with Don Sahlin, were to become the core creative group behind the Muppets. So, you could say that in a small way, this organization helped facilitate the birth of Kermit the Frog and Miss Piggy's lovers' saga.

Lifting the Veil of Economic Depression

Ralph Stevenson raised Leghorn hens with the hope that they would lay bigger and better eggs than other breeds he had tried.

He told his friend Clyde Michael that his laying hens were producing outstanding eggs, so Clyde bought a dozen.

When Clyde had his breakfast the next day, he decided to fry one of the eggs. When he cracked open the egg, three yolks emerged. The odds of that happening are 1 in 25 million.

Clyde happened to be a correspondent for the *Pickaway County News*, so he was quick to describe a special hen

Clyde Michael

on the Stevenson farm. He felt that Stevenson and his hens—especially one in particular—had something to cackle about. This hen, he reasoned, was doing her part to lift the veil of the economic depression by providing a bigger bargain than all the others.

Clashing with Captain Kangaroo.

Clyde and his wife, Vivian, also had something to cackle about. Their daughter Gayle and her husband Doug Anderson moved from South Bloomfield to New York City, where they became early television pioneers. They were hosts of several memorable children's television shows, including *Bonamo, the Magic Clown* and the *Big Top* on CBS.

Both Gayle and Doug were excellent artists. Doug found work illustrating for the *New York Times* and Gayle did technical illustrations. But Doug was also immensely talented as a magician, ventriloquist, and puppeteer. When Captain Kangaroo (Bob Keeshan) was stricken with a heart attack, the producers of the show hired Doug to step in as the Magic Barn Painter while the Captain recuperated. Doug had appeared periodically as that character before and had good reviews for the way he creatively engaged children.

Keeshan heard through the grapevine that one of his sponsors thought Doug was so good that he should permanently replace the Captain. Obviously, that did not sit well with him. When he returned, he ended Doug's association with the show.

While this was a setback for Doug, it was not the end of his career. He became a national television advertising spokesperson

Marionette carved by Doug Anderson

for Black & Decker. Many people also remember him for his national Wendy's commercials, in which he appeared as Dave Thomas's butler, and a local ad campaign for Ohio State Bank, where he portrayed a thrifty Scotsman.

Doug Anderson as the Thrifty Scotsman. Courtesy Doug Anderson Collection

Doug and Gayle (Michael) Anderson as children's television hosts

Doug Anderson as Bonamo the Clown. Courtesy Doug Anderson Collection

Peacock Greeters

While Ashville had a famous rooster greeter in Chic-Chic, the post office in nearby Orient had a pair of exotic peacocks that served this function. The birds would roost on the roof of the post office, and, according to Orient resident Daisy Orsbon, they would come down to just stand in front of the door. Postal officials were unaware of how the birds came to reside there, and residents checked with nearby farms that had

peacocks, but none of the farmers would claim the pair. When the news of this welcoming twosome came to light, WBNS-10TV sent a reporter down to cover the story. They filmed the birds at the post office.

You might ask, "Why would a nesting pair of peacocks be attracted to Orient, Ohio?" Well, after all, in China these birds were a symbol of the Ming Dynasty, representing divinity, rank, power, protection, and beauty. Obviously, these birds from eastern Asia were sent by the goddess Guan Yin to protect the Orient (Post Office)?

Abdominal snowman.

People living in the Orient ZIP Code are evidently quite inventive. There are twenty-seven known patented inventors, and five of them have produced multiple patents. The most prolific of these inventors was George Stanton. George had nine patents issued for devices that pumped fluids.

Perhaps the most unusual patent created by an Orient-area inventor was a snowman mold. Future banking pioneer, Tiney McComb, had seen the poorly shaped snowpeople that children in his neighborhood had sculpted. He watched as children attempted to roll snowballs into much bigger balls and witnessed the hard time they were having trying to lift these heavy balls of packed snow on top of others to make snowpeople.

McComb designed and built a plastic injection mold form that allowed anyone to fill the mold with snow—filling the abdominal cavity first—until the mold was full. The user would unhinge the mold, leaving a perfectly shaped snowman or snowwoman that could then be artistically sculpted. Of course, the rest of the year there would be a snowperson mold taking up valuable real estate in the basement or garage.

The fact that you do not see snowpeople molds when you are out holiday shopping tells you that although it did solve a problem, maybe not all perceived problems need to be solved. While others may search in vain for the abominable snowman, we think we know where to find the abdominal snowman. Look for it in Tiney's old garage.

The Original Spiderman

Marvel Comics' Spider-Man debut came in 1962, but Ashville's Spiderman started spinning spider silk back in the late 1930s.

Dr. John G. Albright, with the help of his brother, Emil, raised spiders to produce crosshairs for optical instruments. In the 1940s they and their spiders went into high gear to produce silk for World War II allied bomb and rifle sights.

Dr. John G. Albright capturing spider silk.

Dr. Albright got into the business of producing spider silk to repair telescopes at the Case School of Applied Sciences, where he was a professor of meteorology, but he and his brother soon became suppliers of spider silk for other universities, surveying equipment manufacturers, and manufacturers of scientific instruments. Their prowess as spider farmers was highlighted in the magazines *The American Surveyor, Flying,* and *Popular Science.*

Albright was an accomplished, patented inventor and was vice president of the National Inventors' Congress. He invented an interruptible circuit and a high-speed method for capturing lightning strikes on film.

It was his expertise in the science of atmospheric lightning that landed him on the front page of the *New York Times* and other major newspapers. The *Associated Press* interviewed him in the wake of the Hindenburg disaster to discover whether it was possible the tragedy might have been caused by lightning. He told them that a static charge or lightning could have indeed doomed the airship.

Fighting the evil weevil.

While Dr. Albright was adept at milking the spider silk from golden garden spiders (*Miranda aurantia*), there was another person from the area that gained national prominence because of his association with bugs. Dr. Thaddeus Hedges Parks grew up on a farm near Ashville. He was fascinated by bugs as a child, so it was not surprising to learn that he wanted to become an entomologist.

What was surprising was that he would become the nation's first USDA Cooperative Extension entomologist. He was a pioneer in pest detection and plant inspection methods. His work recommending practices to keep alfalfa weevils, Mormon crickets, and clover aphids under control is legendary.

During his forty-seven years of public service he wrote more than a thousand popular articles, bulletins, and circulars. He also managed to write 166 scientific publications dealing with insect-related problems.

Field work at Snake Den's center mound, 1897. Courtesy Ohio History Connection

Goodness Snakes Alive

When farmers first started clearing the woodlands east of the Scioto River, they learned about a group of mounds on a high promontory. It wasn't long after clearing the land for farming that the landowners living adjacent to the mounds noticed that their fields would be crawling with snakes about the time they were trying to plow and plant their ground. The large stone mound and a center mound platform were the perfect habitat for snakes to wait out the winter and bring forth their young.

If you had a team of horses pulling your wooden plow and they were spooked by a snake, you might be in a world of hurt—especially if they took off running with you still holding on to the reins.

Supposedly, armed with this knowledge, a farmer named Brown built a high fence around the stone mound and platform during the late winter of 1817. He and neighboring farmers were on the lookout that spring for the snakes to emerge. At the first sign of the snakes, a call went out to all the neighbors. They came with muskets and clubs to kill the serpents, and a slaughter ensued.

In 1897 State Archaeologist Clarence Loveberry and his field crew heard this story and thought it to be an old wives' tale. As they dug into the stone platform, they soon realized after unearthing thousands of snake bones that the site was well named—Snake Den.

It is still not unusual to see a black rat snake emerging from brumation at Snake Den in the Spring.

Loving nature—even snakes.

The people of Central and Southern Ohio owe a debt of gratitude to Clyde Gosnell, Dr. Louise Warner, Dr. Jack Warner, and Gale and David Warner. The Warner family, under the tutelage and inspiration of Gale, developed the highly regarded Stratford Ecological Center in Delaware, Ohio. The center is a working farm that uses sustainable farming practices and engages visitors with ecological learning opportunities.

Louise and Clyde were founding members of the Appalachia Ohio Alliance, a land conservancy and stewardship organization in Southeastern Ohio that has preserved thousands of acres of critical flyway corridors, prairies, and family farms.

Louise and Clyde have also served on the board of the Friends of the Hocking Hills State Park, through which they have raised money for the Raptor Center. They are credited with leading the charge to relocate State Route 664 at Old Man's Cave. The road previously forced visitors to dodge traffic while crossing the road from the parking lot. They also worked with the Friends of the Hocking Hills to spearhead the effort to develop John Glenn Astronomy Park near the Hocking Hills State Park dining lodge.

Ecologists Louise Warner and Clyde Gosnell

Soup of the Day—Coin Collector

Most communities have someone who is an avid numismatist—a coin collector. Ashville had a most unusual one. This interest was not determined until his demise and would *never* have been discovered had his body not been drawn and quartered to supply a local bar owner with stock for soup. Here is the story as it appeared in California's *San Bernardino News* in 1915:

> *Finds Pennies in Turtle*—Ashville, Ohio, July 19.—Roy Bowsher, the local tailor, went fishing last week and caught a turtle, which he sold to C.R. Cook, the proprietor of a saloon. When Cook opened the turtle, preparatory to serving it on his lunch counter, he found 234 pennies in it.

In the early 1900s snapping turtle soup was a favorite meal of President William Howard Taft. Local residents also highly prized it.

While this story may be hard to swallow, remember that recently in Thailand there was a green sea turtle named Banks who swallowed more than nine hundred coins over a period

This restaurant served coin collector soup.

of time while in captivity. Locals believed that throwing loose change to the turtle in her pond would bring a person longevity and good fortune. Unfortunately, it did not bring Banks the turtle good luck because, while five veterinarians operated on her and successfully removed the coins, she died a short time later from blood poisoning.

How the Ashville wild turtle managed to locate and ingest more than two hundred pennies is indeed a mystery. Could it have been fed pennies to increase the purchasing price based on weight? Not likely, because 145 pennies weighed a pound and a live turtle would bring only five cents per pound in 1907. Feeding pennies to a turtle would be a losing proposition.

Serving turtle soup attractively.

Not only did Florence Brobeck know how to prepare turtle soup, she could also tell you the temperature at which to serve it and the proper tureen to serve it in. The *New York Times* best-selling cookbook author grew up on Long Street in Ashville. Her dad was Ashville's first fire chief and a barber.

She was associate editor for the *New York Tribune*'s Institute for Testing (an early forerunner of *Consumer Reports* magazine) and a frequent contributor to *Good Housekeeping, Woman's World,* the *American Magazine, Town & Country, McCall's,* and the *New York Times.* She was also the editor of the *Modern Home News* and the women's editor for the *New York Herald.* But she is best known for teaching Americans how to cook and present food.

The Great Pumpkin

In the vast and fertile grounds of the Midwest there is one pumpkin patch where Linus of *Peanuts* fame would have been able to fulfill his dreams of witnessing the annual return of the "Great Pumpkin." Nearly every year from 1955 to 1976 the Coon Brothers—George, Frank, and Don— won the world-famous heavyweight squash competition at the Circleville Pumpkin Show. Seventeen times during

October 24, 1929, *Pickaway County News*, Frank and Don Coon. Courtesy Ruth Eberts

that twenty-one-year period, their portly produce tipped the scales above all comers.

The brothers began growing prize-winning pumpkins, squash, and other vegetables long before 1955. In 1932 they were winners at both the Ohio State Fair and the Pumpkin Show for the best display of pumpkins and squashes. In 1934

George and Frank Coon with squash, 1960. Courtesy Ruth Eberts

they won first place at the Pumpkin Show for the largest squash.

In 1977 George's son, Mark, continued the tradition his uncles and father started. He entered the Fourth Annual World Series of Pumpkin Growers, which pitted the largest entries from the Circleville Pumpkin Show with those from Half Moon Bay in California. Each community had someone from their community at the other's weigh-in to ensure fairness. Mark's squash entry was nearly double the weight of the largest California challenger, and his Big Max pumpkin was fifty pounds heavier than that of his competitors in Half Moon Bay. The officials at the Pumpkin Show kindly let the officials at Half Moon Bay know that they had been "squashed."

Fun guy with fungi.

Botanical explorer, Kansas's first state botanist, and the Father of American Mycology, Dr. William Ashbrook Kellerman was born in Ashville in 1850. His father, Daniel, was Ashville's first postmaster, and his mother, Idy, was a sister to Mahlon and Absalom Ashbrook— the two men who founded the settlement.

Kellerman was the cofounder and editor of the *Journal of Mycology* (which is still published today) and the *Mycological Bulletin* (mycology is the scientific study of fungi). He also led several scientific botanical expeditions into the Guatemalan jungle during the early 1900s to collect newly identified tropical plant specimens. It was on the 1908 trip that he contracted malaria and died.

For his contributions, botanists named several plants in his honor. Notable among these are a local wild sunflower (*Helianthus X kellermanii*) and Kellerman's begonia (*Begonia kellermanii*). A portion of Kellerman's massive collection is on display at OSU's Bio Museum, and the Ohio State University Herbarium has framed displays that Kellerman assembled for the World's Columbian Exhibition on the walls.

Over My Dead Body

James Short, the first settler in Harrison Township, together with his son Stephen, came to what is now the South Bloomfield area from the state of Delaware. They arrived there and squatted on the land in 1798. They chose land known as the Walnut Plains because it was ready for tilling. When the land was finally for sale in 1801, James rode to Chillicothe to purchase it.

The Twin Elms in South Bloomfield. Courtesy Pickaway County Genealogical Library

James built a log cabin near the old Indian trail, which later turned into the main highway from Franklinton to Chillicothe (we know it today as US Route 23). In his old age he liked to sit in the shade of two elm trees and watch the passing horseback riders and foot traffic. Mr. Short died on August 12, 1816, at the ripe old age of seventy-three.

Around 1830, when the Columbus turnpike was chartered and being built, it was proposed that the elms be removed. This was too much for the local settlers. At the urging of his family, fifteen-year-old Adam Millar grabbed his gun and camped under the trees for several days to make certain the trees were not touched by the turnpike crew. In the end, the Short family donated additional land around the trees for the turnpike with the stipulation that the Twin Elms would continue to stand as long as they were living—as a monument to James Short.

In 1928 the State of Ohio took special care to pave around the elms, which were estimated to be about seven hundred years old. They even enlisted the aid of a tree expert to ensure that the road would not in any way disturb the majestic beauty of the elms. However, the driver of an automobile speeding south on US 23 in the early morning fog of October 19, 1935, did not see the flashing lights that protected the trees. Anthony Hass and Miss Helen Braun died instantly of broken necks as their car smashed into one of the elms. The county commissioners sent a petition to the state to have the trees removed, and so they were taken down months later.

No one thought to take seedlings from the trees to plant near the graves of James Short and Adam Millar. They probably would have liked that.

Big tree hunter.

The Twin Elms were massive and stately trees that one former Ashville resident would like to have seen. Brian Riley is affectionately known as Ohio's Big Tree Hunter. Of the 263 trees documented by the Ohio Department of Natural Resources to be the largest in girth of their species, Riley nominated 125.

Two of the state champions on the list were located in Ashville. Unfortunately, one of those met its demise. It was a catalpa tree that was located near the corner of Madison and Scioto Streets. The huge tree was noted for dropping a massive number of long seed pods that would litter everything under its canopy.

Shot Dead by a Mad Cow

Statistics show that more people are killed by cows every year than by sharks. It is not even close. Deaths by cows are almost four times the number of deaths by shark attack. You should know right now that this story of a former local man's encounter with an angry cow does not have a happy ending.

Ira Cummins had been out hunting with a friend. They were coming home when they met a cow and her calf that should have been heading toward the barn. The two young men undertook the task of driving them back to the barn, but the cow would have none of it.

According to the report, the cow became vicious and charged the two men, knocking Ira to the ground with his gun in hand. When the loaded gun hit the ground it discharged, the buckshot entering his body below the ribs on his left side and lodging in his right lung.

Ira's friend carried the still-conscious man home. He struggled to survive, but thirteen hours later the wounds proved to be fatal.

Sadly for Ira, this is the only time in human history that a bovine shot and killed a human being. This was not premeditated murder—it was manslaughter, plain and simple. But no one alive knows what happened to the cow in question. Did she live out her days on the farm? Was she allowed to have more calves? Did the family continue to milk her or was she immediately taken to be slaughtered?

He got the green light.

Ira Cummins was felled by a cow and Dr. William Ashbrook Kellerman contracted malaria when he was bitten by a mosquito. One local person became a hero in Montana because he died when testing blood samples of tick-bitten individuals who had contracted Rocky Mountain spotted fever.

Dr. Arthur Howard McCray went to Montana in 1919 to take the position of state bacteriologist. While he was engaged in his official duties at his laboratory in Helena, he became infected with Rocky Mountain spotted fever—the very disease he was endeavoring to combat.

Bacteriologist Dr. Arthur H. McCray. Courtesy Montana Board of Health

McCray and others knew that this often-fatal disease was linked to tick bites. The Montana Board of Public Health made this great tribute to him on behalf of the people of that state:

Here Doctor Arthur H. McCray gave his life to save life. Indeed, he saved others, but he himself he could not save. It is heroic, sacrificial, unselfish, and brave. He gave himself completely in his special work. If he could not save himself, he has left a heritage of example, endeavor, and result, that will allow others to save many.

Errol Flynn starred in a 1937 film, *Green Light*, as Dr. Newell Paige, a surgeon who travels to Montana to assist a researcher in Rocky Mountain spotted fever, almost dying when he subjects himself to an experimental serum. The film subplot was loosely based on Dr. McCray's work, and the credits of the movie acknowledge his sacrifice.

The Great Blue Heron

People with koi ponds know that the great blue heron is a highly efficient fish-eating predator that can clean out a pond in no time. Blue herons hunt fish that are difficult to see in lakes, ponds, and rivers that have low or no visibility, so when they see a small crystal-clear pond that is only a few feet deep with brightly colored fish swimming about, they are thinking, "Wow, who provided the buffet?"

Great blues are one of the most successful fish predators around. One trick they use to lure fish to the surface of the water is to regurgitate some of the contents of their stomach into the water, where the fish assume (just guessing) that they just hit the jackpot. That would be their last thought—if they have thoughts.

Observing a blue heron standing in a stream, motionless and ready to strike, can be breathtaking. This tallish bird (about four feet in height) has a whitish head with black plumes that jut out just above and behind its eyes. Its body is brown, black, and white—not blue at all—yet some believe it has sort of an overall bluish-gray appearance.

Ohio's Scenic Rivers license plate was developed to raise funds to help protected species like the blue heron. The plate depicts a heron above a flowing river. Rebecca (Dum) Chambers of Ashville was the graphic artist for the final design.

I Voted.

Thanks to people like Rebecca, entering a contest to design
a graphic that might be used by the State of Ohio is not so
formidable that local people would shy away from it. Teays Valley
High School senior Emily Legg took up a design challenge offered
by the Ohio Secretary of State, who was looking for a new design
for the department's "I Voted" sticker.

When she heard about the contest, she grabbed red and
blue coloring pencils and fleshed out her design. Using the two-
color scheme, she created a design that said, "Ohio Voted," as
well as "I Voted," by highlighting the "I" in Ohio. Her prideful
statement about our state voting also artfully incorporated the
personal statement from individuals who proudly performed their
civic duty.

Emily's 2019 design was chosen over two thousand others
submitted by sixth- through twelfth-grade students in Ohio.

Emily Legg's "I Voted" design with Secretary of State.

Chapter Two

Surprise, Visitors, and Surprising Visitors

Every community in Ohio has surprising stories about local residents that defy rational explanation. Every community also has surprising stories about visitors who, although they may have been present for only a few hours, left their mark—for good or bad.

The Ashville area is no exception. Other visitors have come hoping to take advantage of their welcoming nature. Some left with a pocketful of money while others were arrested or worse. Outsiders have made an impression with their oratory, and some have tested the moral underpinnings of the community.

What makes Ashville different is that there is no other community in Ohio that has confronted theories about Vikings visiting the area or reports that His Satanic Majesty or an alien from outer space paid them a visit.

In John Milton's epic poem *Paradise Lost*, Satan ponders his next step in the Garden of Eden, as shown in this 1866 illustration by Gustave Doré. Ashville's John Milton Long found what many claimed to be the devil in the garden behind his Long Street home.

Ouch!

It was not uncommon in the early part of the twentieth century to read in a farm community's newspaper about an unfortunate hunting accident— usually one hunter unintentionally shot another. Benjamin "Elroy" Dunnick probably wished he was so lucky. No, what happened to poor Elroy would follow him throughout his short lifetime.

Benjamin Elroy Dunnick

The then-fifteen-year-old Dunnick was attempting to climb over a barbed wire fence with his gun in hand. Just as he was about to step over the top, the fence swayed, throwing him backward. Unfortunately, he landed on the muzzle of his gun, which penetrated his rectum to a distance of six inches. As the article in the *Pickaway County News* noted, "The end of the gun was bent, showing heavy contact."

Dunnick recovered sufficiently to return to school in just a few weeks. But that just is not the kind of front-page story you want to see about yourself, because you know your friends will never let you live it down.

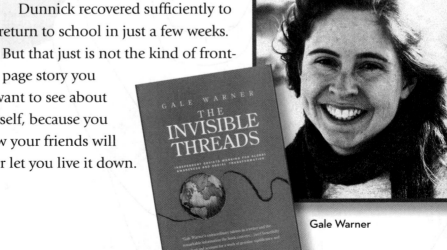

Gale Warner

Gun barrel diplomacy.

Social and environmental activist Gale Warner worked during the Cold War to establish people-to-people lines of communication between American and Soviet citizens. In fact, she wrote two important books on the subject: *Citizen Diplomats: Pathfinders in Soviet-American Relations— and How You Can Join Them* and *The Invisible Threads: Independent Soviets Working for Global Awareness and Social Transformation*. The following is an account of Gale Warner's impactful life from the Stratford Ecological Center's Legacy Series:

Gale and David Kreger were married in 1987, and continued their efforts to end the Cold War by organizing a series of cooperative initiatives between American and Soviet citizens. In order to write a report on a Soviet grassroots effort to stop nuclear testing, Gale managed to slip through Soviet checkpoints in 1989 to visit a 'hot' nuclear underground test site in Kazakhstan. Also in 1989, she and David, along with their Soviet friends, founded an international organization called "Golubka" (meaning "dove" in Russian) to educate people across the Soviet Union on strategies and tools of nonviolence, social and personal empowerment, ecological balance, and the peaceful resolution of conflicts.

It was the morning of August 19, 1991, when Soviet citizens woke up to learn that reformist Mikhail Gorbachev had been overthrown in a coup led by Gennadi Yanaev and other members of the old Soviet guard. But the attempted coup stalled in part because members of Golubka handed out flowers to the young Russian soldiers, placing them in rifle and tank gun barrels. Emboldened by the support of these citizens, Boris Yeltsin defied the leaders of the coup. The tank commanders joined Yeltsin's side and the coup failed.

He Got the Drop on Them

In 1890 an alleged horse thief named Kutz escaped from the Columbus police and headed south. He rode with his guns blazing into South Bloomfield and then to the east through the Village of Ashville, shooting at anyone who ventured out.

Mayor Stephen Fridley

Upon hearing the reports, Stephen D. Fridley, the mayor of Ashville, deputized sixteen men to assist Leander Ward, the town marshal, in the capture of the desperado. This force was thought to be sufficient to capture a criminal the caliber of Jesse James. Unfortunately, Kutz was able to maneuver around Marshal Ward and get the drop on the deputies. He disarmed them all and then amused them by shooting holes in tin cans they were compelled to throw into the air.

This story made its way onto the front pages of newspapers across the nation. The *Cincinnati Enquirer*, for one, noted that after Kutz was done playing with the deputies, he departed town, and the inhabitants were left to wonder about the propriety of paying the deputy marshals for their services. In any event, the town elected Bill Miller the new mayor one month later.

Calaboose calamity.

Newspapers around the country in 1883 reported a story about the Ashville, Ohio, jail burning down with an unfortunate prisoner inside. They related that the prisoner was an umbrella mender from the Dayton Soldier's Home who had a considerable amount of money on his person. He was locked up for being drunk and disorderly by Marshal Will Shoemaker. These papers implied that he was murdered for the money and the building burned to conceal the crime. Local papers like the *Circleville Democrat and Watchman* had a slightly different story:

None of those first at the scene were aware that any person was in the building, and not until it fell, was the horrifying scene presented of a human being burned to death. The body was consumed, except for the backbone, pelvic bones and bowels, which were charred. It was a sickening sight, affecting the most iron nerved. The body lay on the south side of the calaboose, with the head towards the east, where there was a bunk or bench, upon which is supposed to be sleeping.

It is claimed by some that there was evidence a hole about 3x4 feet had been cut into the calaboose, and two or three persons testified to hearing a pounding like noise in that direction. This created the impression that the man had been murdered and the building then fired. There were several rumors that he had exhibited a roll of bills and other money, on Saturday ... The story that the deceased had any considerable money was not sustained with three or four persons testifying that he only had two or three dollars. His remains were buried in the graveyard at Ashville, on Sunday.

The affair is horrible in the extreme, seems to be surrounded by a complete mystery, but no means necessary should be left unemployed to bring light to all the particulars and the offenders... There is a reward of $585 offered.

Although there was an inquest, the cause of the fire was never determined.

Encounter of the Third Kind

This is a copy of a National UFO Reporting Center sighting. It was made by someone years after the actual occurrence. The experience happened to maternal twins that lived at Mann's trailer park near Rickenbacker Airforce Base—several miles north of Ashville. These twins were about nine or ten at the time of the occurrence. They were hanging out at a friend's trailer at about 2:30 in the morning—just a few lots away from their parents' trailer. Here is part of their story:

About the same time my sister says she heard a commotion coming from Rickenbacker. Men were yelling and truck motors were racing. At that moment an apple fell out of our mid-sized apple tree in the yard. We turned around and looked up in the tree. I saw a very small man hunched, crotched down with his very long arms hanging out in front of him, his body was half in the light. His color was bluish grey his legs where silky smooth like a woman's and his hands where funny looking. Not sure why, but I got the impression he meant us no harm and I got the impression we were interrupting something. My sister saw this from her view point. She says she saw a very small man in a gargoyle like stance with his long arms hanging out off his knees. She says his color was dark she did not see him in the light. She says his head was elongated in the back—that is all she can recall of him.

We both saw him. He did not move—he was motionless. Now we were freaking out. We ran to the front again and this time my sister went to the corner of the deck and started crying. I beat on the door and started yelling for dad. This time I could see him through the glass he was asleep in his recliner and did not move. I remember nothing after seeing him asleep. My sister and I only remember waking up the next day in our beds.

A Martian invader lived here.

We have gone through periods of hysterical concern thinking we were about to be invaded by Martians. Now we are living in an age where we are the invaders. Former Ashville resident Dr. Diana Blaney studies geologic processes on planets. She was an investigator on the Mars Science Laboratory (MSL) rovers at the Jet Propulsion Lab.

Her *Phoenix* mission team uncovered a shallow ice table in the northern arctic region of Mars. In the late summer, snowfall and frost blanketed the surface at night. Diana's instruments found that H_2O ice and vapor constantly interacted with the Martian soil.

Diana Blaney's Mars rover model in case

In an article for *Science* magazine, she and her co-scientists reported that the *Phoenix* landing site had aqueous minerals and salts in the soil. They concluded that their formation was likely the result of the presence of water.

Inside Kaiserman's store on Long Street

Sleeping Beauty ... Sort Of

Around 1932 a stranger popped into town. According to author Gale Leatherwood, the stranger found his way to a restaurant on Long Street. Locating the owner, Clyde Brinker, he said, "Sir, I can help your business and bring more people downtown. I will hypnotize myself and lay out in that store window across the street [Kaiserman's store]. I will not go to the bathroom. I will not take food nor water. I will not have a watch with me to tell time. I will not open my eyes. I will be asleep. If you agree, I will hold out my hand at the end of seventy-two hours and you will pay me twenty dollars."

Well, Clyde was one of the best ballyhooers ever for Ashville's downtown businesses—especially his own. He knew a good deal when he saw one, so he agreed and began soliciting the other businesses. He quickly reached his goal (some said he did so without having to put any money into the pot himself) and held the money in escrow for the stranger.

The first twenty-four-hour period brought by a few gawkers, but the next twenty-four had the whole town talking. Many could not believe the feat was possible, so they set up a schedule to watch the gentleman in the window day and night. By the third day, people were elbow to elbow on the sidewalk downtown. Brinker's restaurant was indeed doing a land-office business selling ham sandwiches and hamburgers.

As the four o'clock hour approached, the time when the seventy-two-hour period would be up, people crowded in to see if anything would happen. By now the whole street was

Pete Johnson and Clyde Brinker, men about town who watched the sleeper.

clogged with people. Supposedly at two minutes after four, our sleeping beauty batted his eyes a few times as the crowd began to shout. Then he sat up, shook his head, and held out his hand for the agreed-upon twenty dollars. He got up and was on his way.

There are many examples in the early 1900s of hypnotist showmen placing a local resident into a hypnotic state, in which they would be on display, sometimes for several days, in a local store window. The hypnotist would have the person carried to a local opera house, where he would release the sleeping subject from his or her catatonic state. But the Ashville stranger's self-hypnosis trick is in a class by itself.

Go for it.

If there is one thing that local people with an entrepreneurial spirit learned from Clyde Brinker it was that when you've got a good idea, you should "go for it." That is just what Charlie Fortner did after deciding to move to Hawaii.

He founded Island Page in Honolulu and created the company's Captain Beep Beep marketing campaign. The successful campaign grew the company's sales to more than $1 million. Based on his success, the US Small Business Administration named him its 1998 Young Entrepreneur of the Year.

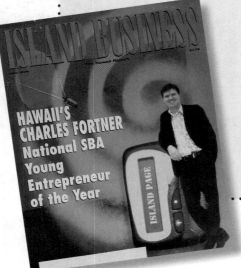

HAWAII'S CHARLES FORTNER National SBA Young Entrepreneur of the Year

Archaeological curator Linda Pansing from Ohio History Connection discusses geologic material from the Snake Den Mounds.

Vikings ... Here?

The local high school mascot is a Viking, and Ashville has an annual Viking Festival that pays homage to the people from Denmark, Norway, and Sweden who, during the period from 700 AD to 1100 AD, would go off on raiding ships. Nearly half a millennium before Columbus "discovered" America, a Viking fleet under Leif Eriksson may have been the first to touch North America. The Norsemen may have established temporary settlements in Newfoundland. There is even inconclusive evidence that they may have smelted bog ore at some of these locations.

Amateur archaeologist Arlington Mallery believed that prehistoric Native Americans in Ohio built and used pit iron furnaces. He became rather famous in central Ohio for suggesting that "Viking iron furnaces" had been discovered in Ross County—clashing with the established view of professional archaeologists. He wrote a book called *Lost America*, in which he classified several Ross County, Ohio, pit furnaces as "Nordic" or "Celtic," pointing to the Norse of Greenland as the source of this technology.

The Snake Den Complex seven miles east of Ashville has a large pit on the center mound in which examples of melted rock were found and cataloged by the 1897 state archaeologist's site investigation. Further study of this rock by Dennison University in 2017 concluded that this was not volcanic rock but rather was created by a man-made process.

Was Mallery correct? Did the Vikings or their old-world technology make it to this area, or did the Native Americans independently develop the technology to create a fire hot enough to melt rock? Although bog ore was found at Snake Den, there was no evidence of iron being smelted. Another fact to consider is that the mounds were constructed hundreds of years before the Vikings were present in North America, so it would seem impossible that the Vikings had anything to do with the ancient Snake Den rock-melting process. Findings like these have been used to largely discredit Mallery's hypothesis.

Viking horde invades Ashville.

Every year since 2004, the Lost Vikings Hoard of Ashville converts the Community Park into an eclectic celebration of living history with a wide collection of spirited reenactors over a two-day event. People enter the event by donating cans of food to the local food pantry. The festival and the food pantry donation entry fee were conceived by Ed Vallette. Ed unexpectedly passed away on May 12, 2014, but his legacy event has continued to grow as an attraction.

While you will not see pillage and plunder, you will encounter a Viking Village encampment and you can participate in building a shield wall and climb aboard a Viking ship. If you come, you will see jousting and can observe medieval craftspersons creating shields and forging weaponry. You can also bargain for handcrafted items that you just will not find  anywhere else. The Vikings are a hearty bunch who like sweet and savory food, so the aromas coming from the festival are bound to entice your taste buds.

The event usually happens on a Saturday and Sunday in late April from 10:00 a.m. to 5:00 p.m. You will want to go to the festival's website or Facebook page for more information.

The Silver-Tongued Orator

William Jennings Bryan came to town on August 2, 1918, as the featured speaker for the Chautauqua that was being held at Hoover's Woods (just south of the Harrison Township Fire Department on SR 752). He stayed at the Ashville Hotel, which had never had a more high-profile patron.

At four o'clock in the afternoon, unaided by a microphone, he began. From a four-foot-high platform, his rich and grand voice reached everyone in the five-acre Chautauqua grounds. Years later some locals recounted that you could hear his booming voice even a mile away.

Bryan had just come from petitioning the US Congress to enact a prohibition on the sale of liquor during a time of war. Twelve states had already ratified national prohibition, but he suggested to the Agricultural Committee that the country's war effort would be more productive if worker access to intoxicating liquors was removed. Bryan spoke to the assembled crowd at Ashville about the need to pursue prohibition.

William Jennings Bryan at the Ashville Hotel

The speaker has spoken.

William Jennings Bryan was not the only colorful national orator of note, dignitary, or politician to make their case to the people of Ashville. Arizona Senator Henry Ashurst came to town in the early 1900s. Ashurst was a US senator from the year Arizona became a state in 1912 until he was defeated in 1940. The *New York Times* said of him:

> *Sheer eloquence is best personified in the present Senate by Ashurst of Arizona—the debonair, balm-tongued chairman of the Senate Judiciary Committee. Without losing one whit of his eloquence, or missing or misquoting a classical phrase, Ashurst can run the range from buffoonery to some of the most challenging remarks heard in Congress.*

Senator Henry Ashurst

He said of himself:

> *I love auriferous words, and nothing delights me more than to pluck gems from the dictionary that otherwise might never see the light of day.*

Other dignitaries include Seaborn Wright—a recognized leader of the prohibition forces in the South and a progressive candidate for governor of Georgia—a position he did not win. Mrs. Robert LaFollette (Belle Case LaFollette) was a progressive speaker for women's rights.

Belle Case La Folliette

Presidential candidate and progressive governor of Ohio James M. Cox spoke to local residents several times including 1920—the year he was the Democratic nominee for president. He was defeated by fellow Ohioan Warren G. Harding. Cox's running mate was Franklin D. Roosevelt.

James M. Cox

John Milton Long's house on Long Street in Ashville
Right: Author Tiffany McDaniel

A Visit from the Devil

It was a hot August day in 1909 when "John Milton" Long went out to hoe the garden behind his home. He was startled to find a curious looking toad—or was it? He described it as having a toad belly and legs, but its back and, more prominently, its head were covered with spike-like horns. It had a toad mouth and very small eyes, but unlike a toad it had a rather long slender tail.

The editor of the *Pickaway County News* saw the animal, as did many others in town. He was moved to say, "Many who have seen it think it a splendid imitation of 'His Satanic Majesty' and even accuse its discoverer, Mr. Long, of making an effort to 'raise the devil' in his end of town."

This was obviously not a toad, but a horned lizard. Its habitat was not central Ohio but rather the southwest United States, so it is curious how it came to be a resident of Mr. Long's garden.

Ironically, award-winning Ohioana author and former Little Walnut resident Tiffany McDaniel wrote her acclaimed novel, *The Summer that Melted Everything*, based on the premise that the devil was invited to visit a small town, unleashing tragedy. Each chapter was prefaced by a line from English poet John Milton's epic poem *Paradise Lost*. She had no prior knowledge of Ashville's "John Milton" Long or the devil that visited him.

Paradise lost, connection found.

Another irony not known to Ms. McDaniel was that one of the foremost American Milton scholars in the early twentieth century was Evert Mordecai Clark, who was born near Ashville in 1897. He was raised on a farm in eastern Madison Township.

Clark was professor emeritus of English at the University of Texas. He studied at Yale University, earning a BA in 1905 and a PhD in English in 1911. He also served as chairman of the University of Texas English Department from 1921 to 1923 and 1929 to 1934.

Clark edited Milton's *The Ready and Easy Way to Establish a Free Commonwealth* (a popular book, with fourteen editions published between 1915 and 2008). He also published:

- *English Literature: The Seventeenth Century*
- "Milton and the Warfare of Peace"
- "Milton and Wither"
- "Milton's Abyssinian Paradise"
- "The Kinship of Hazlitt and Stevenson"
- "Milton's Earlier 'Samson'"

Are They Ever Ashamed?

It is not often that a nudist colony comes to visit a community, but that is what happened in 1938. A carnival attraction at the Ashville Fourth of July announced that for only a dime, one could visit a nudist colony behind the canvas walls of the tent. The prurient interests of every male must have been stirred by the painting of a partially nude woman turned artfully so her breasts were revealed. The sign above her portrait read, "Are They Ever Ashamed?"

The famous artist and photographer Ben Shahn, who took an often-repurposed photograph of this attraction, must have been amused to see no one near the entrance. Who would dare let his curiosity get the better of him—especially in the daylight?

Nudist colony ready for the crowds at the Ashville Fourth of July. Courtesy Farm Security Administration

We can only assume that the stage performers offered up some enticement that caused brave characters to step forward—most likely wondering after they spent their money if it was all worth it.

Over the years, there have been a few other scurrilous attractions at the Ashville Fourth of July celebration that exposed a little more of the female form than local morals would have allowed. Usually these were shut down, but not until the operators had already made some money.

You ain't seen nothing yet.

There are pamphlets advertising the Ashville Fourth of July going back to 1905, but it wasn't until the Ashville Community Club was formed that it gained status as a true festival. They adopted a constitution and bylaws with the express purpose of "making the community a better place to live."

The first president was attorney G. W. Morrison; the first vice president, G. A. Hook. Ed Schlegel was named secretary and Frank Hudson was appointed treasurer. The executive committee consisted of E. A. Snyder, J. B. Snyder, D. H. Squire, Rev. Chandler, and E. W. Seeds.

Contestant winners for Miss Ashville Fourth of July. Courtesy Ashville Community Club

In 1928 the community had a splendid parade, but the Community Club decided to take this event and make it much bigger. They told people in town that "you ain't seen nothing yet." They were thinking big. They purchased a large display of colorful fireworks and they used the Ashville Community Band to ballyhoo the celebration by holding concerts in all the neighboring villages and towns. They booked some attractions and arranged for an all-star baseball game between Ashville and Circleville.

In 1930 the one-day festival added more free acts and carnival rides in the village park. The club expected a mammoth crowd, and that is what they got, with an estimated twelve thousand people visiting the park grounds. In the years that followed, the club introduced fried fish sandwiches "as big as your hand." These were fried in a small metal pan. The club typically fries more than six thousand pounds of fish during the festivity.

Today the celebration takes place over multiple days and includes a Little Miss and Mister parade, a Miss Fourth of July parade, and a huge Fourth of July Parade.

Smile ... You're on Candid Camera

In 1938 the Farm Security Administration sent social activist and artist Ben Shahn to the Midwest to capture farmers and small-town residents coping with the Great Depression. Shahn wanted to catch people in activities when they were unaware that they were being photographed, so he developed a right-angle camera. This camera allowed him to act like he was photographing something in front of him, but in actuality the lens on the front of his camera was fake. The working lens was on the side, and he was careful to hold it so his fingers would not get in the way.

Shahn was in Ashville for the town's Fourth of July celebration. He took photos of people dancing and standing in line to watch a wrestling match and the carnival midway advertising ten-cent entry to see a nudist colony. He took photos of people eating fish sandwiches and watching a mobile radio show.

Sherwood Anderson

Local people would never have known about the photos, except one of them appeared in a book by Sherwood Anderson. The iconic shot showed three women standing together.

The federal government was not the only organization drawn to Ashville to capture the Fourth of July spirit. In 1967 the *New York Times* sent award-winning photographer Patrick A. Burns—best known for his images of the welcoming parade for the first men on the moon and of the spontaneous celebration in Times Square on V-J day—and author Lisa Hammel to witness the festival. Pulitzer Prize-winning author Michael Vitez, from the *Philadelphia Inquirer*, covered the local celebration with staff photographer Michael Perez in 2002.

Hammel's article noted:

From the surrounding counties, other parts of the state—even from far away as Florida and California—sisters, brothers, parents, aunts, uncles, cousins and grandchildren descend on Ashville households to see the parade, to visit and to partake of a noontime picnic lunch, whose menu is as ritualized on the Fourth of July here as turkey and fixings are in November.

Vitez and Perez were off on a road trip across America when they stopped in Ashville. They followed local community news writer Rose Jamison to the start of the 73rd Ashville Fourth of July Festival. Vitez wrote:

Rose sang the patriotic medley of songs with all of her might at Sunday morning's Community Worship Celebration, right here in the town park under shady oaks, to open the Ashville Fourth of July Celebration. Ashville, a farming town of 2,500 people, claims to have the oldest four-day Fourth of July festival in Ohio.

Little Chicago

People have often wondered how the north end of the Village of Ashville came to be known as "Little Chicago." It was indirectly given this moniker by the editor of the *Pickaway County News*, G. B. Stoker. Seems there was a bit of a gun battle and a car chase through the whole town. The battle royale started late in the night on Monday, August 25, 1930, and extended into the early morning hours of the next day.

Here is how Stoker described the event:

> *The Village of Ashville has now taken its place among the headliners and hereafter will be known as Little Chicago . . . Some of our old residents thought that the British were coming . . . Some say we have within our city limits developed two factions which are bitter rivals in the bootleg business. Others claim the battle was staged by foreign racketeers. Be it this or that, we know there were two machines, one chasing the other, and the occupants of each car were firing rapidly at each other. Several shots were exchanged in the downtown section, two of which were fired near our marshal's home, while others were heard in different sections of town as the*

autos raced madly about . . . The question we all want to ask is, "Where did they bury the dead?" No bodies were discovered scattered over town anyplace Tuesday, nor could we find any blood had been shed.

It was after this event that official maps of the town labeled the unincorporated portion of the village north of town where some bootlegger activity originated as "Little Chicago." This was codified on maps and remained the name of the place even after it was incorporated into the rest of Ashville.

Teetotalers and bootleggers.

Young Freddie Powell proudly signed his name to a vow of temperance not to let his lips touch intoxicating beverages until he reached eighteen years of age. This would not be easy in a town that had more beer joints than churches.

The fight for and against the prohibition of alcohol played out in communities like Ashville, Commercial Point, and Orient in many different ways from the early 1900s until Prohibition ended. From 1920 to 1933 there might be a local Woman's Christian Temperance Union meeting on a Sunday afternoon and on a weekday afternoon the local marshal might be coordinating raids against moonshiners to bust up a still or crashing a bootlegging party on Saturday night.

The General

Of all the famous short-term visitors to Ashville, the *General* is the only one that was central to both a national historic Civil War event (Andrews' Raid, also known as the Great Locomotive Chase) and a star of Buster Keaton's silent film comedy masterpiece *The General*.

James J. Andrews, a civilian scout for the Union Army, sought out volunteers from Ohio's 2nd, 21st, and 33rd Infantry units

to join him on a daring raid to commandeer a Confederate train outside Atlanta and head north to Chattanooga, Tennessee—doing as much damage to the supply lines as possible on the way. The raid began on April 12, 1862, when the *General* stopped so its crew and passengers could get breakfast at the Lacy Hotel in Big Shanty (now Kennesaw). The raiders took the *General* and three boxcars and left the passenger cars behind.

The train's conductor, William Fuller, realized what was happening and immediately gave chase with two others—at first on foot and then by handcar. The raiders made the mistake of not destroying a locomotive that was on the side track, and Fuller and his compatriots used it to get even closer. Eventually, the raiders' luck ran out when the *General* ran out of fuel—just eighteen miles from their destination.

The National Cemetery at Chattanooga, Tennessee, is home to a special monument to the Andrews' Raid participants. As superintendent of the Chattanooga National Cemetery, former Ashville resident Captain John Thomas took special care of the

monument. He was also a volunteer in Ohio's 22nd Infantry during the Civil War.

Eight of the raiders, including James Andrews, were tried and hanged by the Confederate Army in Atlanta. After the war, the United States reburied their remains in a semi-circle at the Chattanooga National Cemetery. In 1891 a granite monument was erected that displayed the names of twenty-two of the participants. On top of this memorial is an unusual bronze likeness of the *General*. The *General* itself is now housed at the Southern Museum of Civil War and Locomotive History, located in Kennesaw near where the Great Locomotive Chase began.

I will wait right here until I hear from you,
John

Moral Victory?

The Waterloo Wonders were the darlings of the basketball world in 1934 and 1935. The team's coach found a starting five from a pool of twenty-five males in the Waterloo school. He developed them into a powerhouse. None of the five was taller than six feet, but they absolutely destroyed other small-town teams and played an entertaining style of basketball unknown at that time. They took hook shots and made full-court passes. They did blind passes and trick plays and made artful layups that would spellbind spectators.

It wasn't just small-town teams that they were beating. They posted victories over big-city Class A schools and even beat Rio Grande College twice and a talented Marshall University freshman team on its way to the 1934 and 1935 Class B championship. Waterloo's record during those two years was an astounding ninety-seven wins and three losses.

On January 18, 1935, Ashville hosted the Wonders from Waterloo. Needless to say, the Ashville gym was packed to the brim for this contest. The Ashville Broncos had a 3–2 lead early in the contest and the crowd had visions of an upset. But alas, that was not to be. The Wonders put on a clinic and produced a final score of 43–22. The local newspaper was content to say that Ashville managed to gain a moral victory despite the final score.

The next year, the team from Waterloo had lost three of their starters to graduation and one joined this group on a barnstorming basketball tour. The return match with Ashville was no contest. Ashville won 42–18.

We also kicked butts.

The number of teams and players from the Ashville area that have distinguished themselves in sports is astounding. There are simply too many state champions, state recordholders, semi-pro teams, all-stars, hall of famers, and NCAA college champions in nearly all sports to give adequate praise and attention here, but if someone wants to write a book, here is a start:

2015 State Champion, Girls Softball
2016 State Runner-Up, Girls Softball
State Wrestling Champ, Mike Wilson
State 880 Meters Champion, Perri (Martin) Lehman
State Shot Put Champion, Ray Odaffer
State High Jump Champion, Krystal (Dowdy) Reeb
State High Jump Champion, Elmer "Red" Mallory
State Pole Vault Champion and OHSAA Coaches Hall of Fame,
    Mike Hagley
State High Jump Champion, Glenn Kraft
Ohio Collegiate Hammer Throw Record, J. Stanley Stevenson
1945 Men's Class B State Basketball, Third Place
2011 OASSA Division 1 State Champion, Cheerleading
2014 OASSA Division 2 State Champion, Cheerleading
2018 OASSA Division 2 State Champion, Cheerleading
2019 OASSA Division 2 State Champion, Cheerleading
1971 All-State Basketball Team, Van Gregg
Drake University All-Decade Basketball, Harold Ebert
Morehead State Basketball, Bob Hoover
Women's AAU All-American Basketball, Mindy Fusetti
Wilmington College 2004 NCAA Division 3 Women's Champion,
    Samantha Hood
Ashland University 2016 NCAA Division 2 Women's Champion,
    Baylee Kuhlwein
Capital University 1994 and 1995 NCAA Division 3 Champion,
    Patricia Fortner

1945 All-State Basketball, Richard Messick

Ohio State University Basketball, Richard Hudson

Ohio University Basketball and OHSAA Coaches Hall of Fame, Russell Gregg

Rio Grande Athletic Hall of Fame, Holly Hastings

Norwood University Basketball Hall of Fame, Tom Rathburn

Central District Basketball Tournament Scoring Recordholders (Tie), Dale Lambert and Van Gregg

1990 All-State Basketball Team, Amy Colborn

1972 NCAA Division 1 Football Scoring Champion, Harold "Champ" Henson

University of Miami Soccer, Steve Cummins

LeMoyne College NCAA Faculty Representative and MIT Crew member, William V. Miller

Notre Dame Associate Athletic Director, Claire Leatherwood

Northwestern University Chairman of Health and Physical Education Department, Walter H. Gregg

State Championship Coach Brenna Giesige

Van Gregg shoots from twenty-two feet. Courtesy Clemson University

Samantha Hood, NCAA Division III National Championship, Wilmington College. Courtesy Wilmington College

Baylee Kuhlwein (10), Ashland University, 2016-2017 National Champions

Bob Hoover (21), Morehead State College, 1963 Conference Championship

Mindy Fusetti at The Ohio State University

Patricia Fortner, Capital College, 1994 Division III National Champions

A mannequin of the Headless Deaf Woman at Ohio's Small Town Museum is there to warn people to be vigilant when crossing the railroad tracks before daylight.

Chapter Three

After Life

People forget that Ohio's greatest inventor, Thomas Edison, had plans to build a machine to communicate with the dead. Ohioans love to seek out haunted places, including the Ohio Statehouse, where it is claimed the ghost of Abraham Lincoln occasionally appears.

The Ashville area does not take a back seat to any other Ohio community when it comes to apparitions, ghoulish specters, and bizarre funereal practices. People claim to have seen reddish orbs at the Cholera Cemetery or have been scared nearly to death at the sight of the headless deaf woman haunting the N&W railroad tracks or heard screams of a ghostly mule team at Stage's Pond.

If Edison had successfully developed his spirit phone, the people of Ashville would no doubt like to speak to the headless deaf woman (not sure how to communicate with a headless spirit who was deaf when she was alive). The people of South Bloomfield would like to know whose partial body was found in Nate Darling's attic. Most importantly, area residents would like to know the reasoning behind digging up body parts of a deceased person's family members to be buried with the body.

The "Blue Death" Cholera Cemetery

There are various stories about so-called ghostly apparitions associated with a cemetery on the Peters family farm. Stories

abound about unusual red orbs floating about the site and shadowy figures. There have also been accounts of bloodcurdling screams coming from that plot of land.

This cemetery was established by the Renick family (one of the earliest white settlers that owned farmland here about the time Ohio became a state). Today it is known as the Harrison Township Cholera Cemetery

because it was the supposedly the final resting place for a number of canal workers who contracted cholera. The "Blue Death" caused a person's skin to turn bluish-gray from extreme loss of fluids.

Around 1830 the Ohio and Erie Canal was being constructed in northern Pickaway County immediately adjacent to this cemetery. Because canals provided a relatively stagnant source of water that carried human feces from cities, they allowed cholera to fester. As a result of drinking this stagnant water, canal workers sometimes died from this illness. It was a common local saying that an Irishman was buried for every mile of canal constructed here.

The horror of cholera.

People who contracted cholera generally suffered from severe diarrhea (producing three to five gallons of diarrhea per day), vomiting, and cramps. Those with this illness often died from dehydration within a few hours or days after the symptoms first appeared. The unquenchable thirst from dehydration led victims to scream for water. In the final stages, the victims would writhe in extreme pain with uncontrollable spasms. Before the Civil War, doctors would often treat cholera with something called calomel, which contained mercury. Those who survived cholera would sometimes suffer from mercury poisoning, and many died from their intended cure.

45th Infantry Regiment

Death by cholera was indeed terrifying, but quick. It was nothing like the dysentery and typhoid deaths that awaited local lads captured during the Civil War.

Privates Adam Beers and Joseph Harlor from Scioto Township died at the notorious Andersonville Prison. Privates James Tool (Toole) from Scioto Township and Elisha Webb from Ashville died at the despised Libby Prison in Richmond.

All three of the Scioto Township privates were members of Company A in the 45th Regiment, which was organized in August of 1862. In 1863 their regiment pursued Colonel Scott through Eastern Tennessee. It was there on November 13 that the Union's cavalry dismounted, leaving Company A without immediate support. They were overrun by the enemy, and one hundred men, including these three, were taken prisoner. They had every reason to believe they would be treated humanely. They were not, but then being a prisoner of war for either side was life threatening.

Libby Prison

World's Largest Woman (and Ghost)

The World's Largest Woman—Catharine Scholey—lived with her husband William on Walker Road near Commercial Point. At the time she died, she was under the management of Col. Wood's Museum in Chicago and had been previously on exhibit in New York City, Philadelphia, Chicago, and other major cities during the late 1830s and early 1840s.

Catharine (Learch) Scholey was born in 1816 in Salem County, New Jersey, and moved to Ohio. It was here that news of her purported weight and girth reached the famed exhibitor, Col. J. H. Wood. Wood had a large museum of unusual attractions in Chicago, and traveling exhibitions as well. Mrs. Scholey's weight and life story were so compelling that she became a star attraction for his franchise. Her purported weight of 760 pounds was pronounced on marketing banners outside every venue she attended.

Catharine Scholey's rocking chair

It is claimed by people living in Greenwich, New Jersey, that after her death, her obese ghost returned to her hometown, where she wanders the street at night, looking for a little snack. Not to worry, according to the author of *Haunted New Jersey*, Patricia A. Martinelli—"Her ghost waddles along so slowly that you can easily outrun it."

Headless deaf woman.

Area residents do not have to worry about an obese ghost haunting New Jersey. They have their own specter that hangs around the N&W railroad tracks.

It was the late 1950s when the station master at the Ashville depot was peering down the tracks for the early morning passenger train to arrive. The morning darkness was just starting to dissipate. As he looked down the rails, he thought for a moment he saw the figure of a headless woman hovering around the side track. He looked again and it was gone. Years later, a horrifying story from an 1880s Circleville newspaper was found. It read:

The woman killed by the cars at Ashville last Tuesday afternoon was Mrs. Louise Perry of this city (Circleville), daughter of Mrs. Jackson. She was on her way to visit her sister Mrs. Weider at Ashville. The freight train had pulled away from the depot and she started to walk down the siding on which it was.

Being deaf she did not hear it coming back nor the cries of two women who saw her. A brakeman also saw her, and shouted, but in an instant more the train struck her, her severed head bounded into the air, and her poor body was mangled beneath the cars. Never will that sight be forgotten by those who saw it but could do nothing to prevent, or by anyone who beheld the ghastly remains.

If you live in Ashville, please do be careful when crossing the N&W tracks—especially early in the morning. Remember to give anyone or anything standing in the tracks the right of way.

Screaming Mules at Stage's Pond

Those familiar with the Stage's Pond State Nature Preserve may not be aware of the horrific event that visited this normally quiet kettle lake back in the 1880s. Author Jannette Quackenbush tells the ghastly tale of a late summer storm:

A farmer who lived across Ward Road [just west of Stage's Pond] was taking in hay. A storm blew across the fields and he ran to get out of the rain. Lightning bolted across the sky along with an explosion of thunder right after. The wagon team he was using to take in the hay bolted down over the road, across the muddy land around Stage's Pond. Straight into the marshy, quick-sand-like muck they went, mired and fighting until they sank so deep they could not be retrieved.

They say that sometimes after a late-evening lightning storm, you can still hear the mule team smashing their hooves on the ground leading to the pond. You can hear the sound of something crashing into the boggy marshland and the terrified banshee-like screams of the team fighting to free themselves.

You can't help but scream.

Few people can match Arron Kinser's film work when it comes to producing spine-tingling, scary videos and movies. Former Teays Valley graduate Kinser has been acting in, directing, and producing video and film projects in Hollywood for more than two decades. In 2016 he starred in the horror flick *Cruel Will*. The feature film won the RIP Horror Film Festival.

He has worked with Jim Carrey, Kevin Smith, Giancarlo Esposito, Trevor Howard, and a bevy of other film actors and directors. Today he has a recurring role in the TV series *86 Zombies*.

When it comes to natural disasters . . .

Sometimes horror comes from nature's fury and not from some imagined supernatural vendetta against the living. Ashville's Doran Topolosky was tasked by the Department of Defense with shooting footage of various natural disasters—especially floods. But he would tell you that the most hair-raising work he performed was documenting hurricane disasters. His public domain stock footage of disasters like Hurricane Betsy regularly appeared in TV shows and movies like 1974's made-for-TV movie *Hurricane*, which starred Larry Hagman.

Detached Body Part Burials

Archaeologists were called on to investigate a prehistoric burial site found on the grounds of the state corrections training academy at Orient, Ohio. What they found remains one of the biggest mysteries in Ohio archaeology. They were called to the grounds when Mount Sterling Police Chief Chris Carty noticed some loose bones being dug out of an embankment that was to be used for a shooting range.

Archaeologists identified the remains of about twenty individuals representing adults, children, and adolescents who had been dismembered and distributed across twelve burial pits.

Forensic archaeologist Cheryl Johnston

Cheryl Johnston, an archaeologist and the project chief, said, "There's a lot of weird stuff like two people in one grave pit with no heads. There's also the skeleton of a child placed on a set of arms which seem to be cradling it, but the rest of the adult is not there. Nobody's seen anything like this before." There is also a burial that has arms from two different bodies arranged around each side of an artifact, as if it was being handed off in an exchange.

The archaeologists surmised that the people who performed the burials were not being grotesque or engaging in some brutal practice. They believe it was more likely a respectful way to be left for the afterlife, connected to others in your group.

Skeleton in the attic.

We can question why people from an ancient culture might have detached body parts, but it would be downright cringe-worthy to think that could happen in the modern era. Unfortunately, that is what happened in 1905.

Nate Darling of South Bloomfield decided to hire a carpenter to find the source of a leak in his newly purchased home and fix it. The worker climbed into the attic of the small home only to be startled by what appeared to be the skeleton of a man. It wasn't a full skeleton—just the lower half—but it was disturbing because the skin and ligaments were still attached to the detached body.

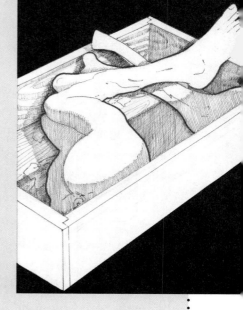

Now, this ghastly find was cause for considerable excitement in the small village. People wondered where was the other half of the corpse. Who might this person have been? Could this have been a crime? Why would anyone be storing the bottom half of a corpse? Should it be given a burial? Were there any members of their community who had mysteriously vanished?

The authorities were never able to fully answer these questions. They investigated who had previously lived in the house, but no evidence of foul play was ever determined. Mr. Darling, however, did eventually get his roof fixed.

The Great Tribute

From coast to coast and from London to Berlin in Europe, people in 1897 were reading about the discovery in Central Ohio of the cremated remains of a great ancient leader of the mound builders. Whoever this person was, the ancient people must have held this person in

The 1897 field work at Snake Den uncovered a large supply of geologic specimens. Courtesy Ohio History Connection

high esteem—the body was buried under a large collection of unusual geologic specimens and man-made utilitarian artifacts used in everyday life.

There were fifty-five heavy cannonball-like concretions placed above this person's final resting place. Interspersed between these spherical deposits were dozens of coral fossils, pestles, hammerstones, crinoid casts, and plummets. They had also placed colored polished pebbles, a quartz crystal, a celt, bog ore, and many other unusual types of sedimentary, metamorphic, and igneous rock specimens. Of course, the discovery of the five silver nuggets in a stone container in the midst of all of this large cache of items also garnered interest from the press, but the headlines across the Western world seemed to focus less on the treasure and more on the apparent fact that these ancient mound-building people practiced cremation. Here is a typical headline from Seattle:

> *The* Seattle Post-Intelligencer. *The Ancients Practiced Cremation—Burned Bones of a Great Chief Unearthed—Students of Archaeology Amazed—Five Large Nuggets of Silver In The Same Mound With The Bones—New Facts for Science.*

The great geologist.

Clarence Loveberry took the geologic specimens from Snake Den to Dr. Edward Francis Baxter Orton Sr., who was the state geologist and the president of the Geological Society of America. When Orton saw the wide variety of fossils and geologic material, he jokingly exclaimed that this must be the cache of a great ancient geologist.

John Adams Bownocker was born near St. Paul, Ohio, on March 11, 1865. As a young man, he heard Dr. Orton give a lecture in his community and decided that he should attend The Ohio State University under the tutelage of Dr. Orton. Bownocker was

Geologist John A. Bownocker. Courtesy Ohio State University

encouraged to enter the field of geology and received his doctorate in that field in 1897 (the same year Dr. Clarence Loveberry got his doctorate in veterinary science at OSU).

Bownocker was named the state geologist in 1906 and remained in that post for twenty-two years. He was also the chairman of the Department of Geology from 1919 until his death in 1928. He published a geological map of Ohio in 1920 that was considered to be of such high quality that it was not replaced until 2006.

There is a medal given in his name each year to outstanding geophysical scientists. The 2018 recipient of the Bownocker Medal was Kevin Trenberth, an expert on global warming and a member of the Nobel Peace Prize-winning Intergovernmental Panel on Climate Change.

Facedown Burial

Dr. Clarence Loveberry had his archaeological fieldwork team cut into the clay mound at the Snake Den Complex to determine if it was a burial mound. Despite the fact that looters had dug several feet deep into the center of the mound, they did not reach the bottom layer. It was there that Loveberry's crew located the remains of eight individuals, one of whom was a child.

Artist's depiction of the Snake Den discoveries, from the St. Paul *Globe*.

There were not many artifacts found with the remains, although there were a few high-quality artifacts with the child. But that is not what puzzled the archaeologist. He noted that one of the burials was a rare facedown interment. While facedown burials in Hopewell mounds are unusual, there is no way to determine whether the Hopewell attached any meaning or sacred purpose to such a practice. It is clear that the facedown interment at Snake Den was deliberate.

In some cultures, being buried facedown shows a sign of disrespect. There is, however, no evidence that the Hopewell practiced this as a way to denigrate or scorn the individual being interred.

Face down a mob.

Samuel Ritter Peters, the distinguished US Congressman from Kansas, grew up on a farm in eastern Walnut Township. Prior to serving in Congress, he was a district judge over nineteen practically lawless counties of Central and Southwest Kansas. It was in this capacity that he faced a most difficult situation. He was a judge at Medicine Lodge, Kansas. Here is a transcript of what happened:

Judge Peters got word that a mob had been formed to take a convicted horse thief away from the sheriff and hang him. Judge Peters was determined to stand for the majesty of the law and had the horse thief brought to his room in the hotel, armed himself and then sent for a rough character in Medicine Lodge to join him in protecting the horse thief.

It was some period of the night that the rough character informed the judge that it was not really necessary to sit up any longer because as he was the man who had gotten the mob up and they would not act without him.

Peters always denied that he invited the Medicine Lodge character knowing he was the instigator. Still, it proved to be a worthy strategy, as the mob stood down and the horse thief was sent to prison still amongst the living.

When Life Gives You Formaldehyde

Until the 1800s, wild eastern oysters were typically harvested and eaten only where they were found. Since oysters do not preserve long once out of their shells, oysters harvested from Chesapeake Bay rarely made it further than could be transported in a day. Nineteenth-century advancements in food preservation and transportation transformed the oyster industry. Newly built railways connected the coast with inland cities and made it possible to ship oysters further west.

John W. Messick went to the Scioto Valley Railroad office and sent a telegraph to a supplier in the east for two barrels of fresh oysters packed in ice. John was a prosperous store owner on Main Street in the newly formed railroad boomtown of Ashville. People in Ashville, like many others in central Ohio, found that oysters cost half as much as beef per pound. They were used to add bulk to more expensive dishes such as meat pies.

The day came when the oysters arrived at the station and would be delivered to Mr. Messick's store and placed on ice. John noticed the barrels containing the oysters had an unusual odor, so he opened one immediately. To his surprise, there were no oysters in the barrel—just embalming fluid.

Well, what to do? Since the closest funeral parlor was in South Bloomfield, John thought this was a fortuitous sign. He became the town's first undertaker.

Paraskevidekatriaphobia -13.

You could say that John Messick turned his bad luck into something good. In a strange way, you could say that local funeral director Edward Schlegel, the successor to John, turned fear of bad luck into something memorable.

In general, area children know that they should not cross the path of a black cat, step on cracks, break a mirror, spill salt, or walk under a ladder—it's bad luck. Similarly, when hanging a horseshoe, it must be done so the open end is at the top so it catches and retains good luck. Most of these superstitions are viewed by local adults as just frivolous fallacies designed to entertain or scare youth. However, there is one local superstition that really held sway with older folks. Never do anything important on the 13th of the month—especially if the 13th is a Friday.

Knowing how people feel about the number 13, it is perhaps a little bit macabre that when the Ashville Citizen's Telephone Company was formed and provided numbers to its first customers, they gave the town funeral home, operated by Mr. Schlegel, the number 13. If you needed his services for any reason, including an ambulance ride to the hospital, you had to dial 13 on your phone.

The Contrarian

George (G. W.) Brown rode with Buffalo Bill during the Civil War. Before that, he fought in the Mormon-Indian Wars in the Utah Territory with the 10th Infantry and worked on cattle ranches in Colorado and Nebraska. He suffered severe wounds during both of these wars. By all accounts, whatever suffering he endured from his wounds was nothing compared to the

George W. Brown

emotional hardship of his early life in the frontier wilds of Minnesota. His father died when he was three years old and his mother died when he was only nine. He joined with a couple of trappers and learned how to survive in the wilderness.

Several years after the war he found himself in Pickaway County. He courted and married the widow Hannah Decker in 1877. They moved to Conneautville, Pennsylvania, but returned to build the first home in Pickaway County to have steam heat, running water, and indoor toilets. The home was located on Duvall Road east of Duvall.

G. W. was generally polite, well spoken, and thoughtful. However, he would engage in heavy drinking in local Ashville and Circleville bars, which led to his boasting of his various adventures and was sometimes followed by brawling and jail time. It was during one such episode that he shot and killed an unarmed man in a Circleville bar. G. W. died before his case could be decided.

He had purchased a plot for Hannah and his final resting place in the Fernwood Cemetery, near Lockbourne. He thumbed his nose at the convention that Christians should be buried with their heads to the west and their feet to the east, so at the final tribulation of Christ they would already be facing toward His coming. This is more tradition than it is biblical, but everyone did it for that reason.

George Brown's dog, Dan

George and Hannah are both buried with their feet to the north and their heads to the south. He could not be buried with his beloved dog, Dan, so he had a statue made that was placed at the foot of their graves.

Some people thought George wanted to be buried facing north because he was a loyal unionist—or maybe he just liked being different.

Death of an era?

Believe it or not, there was a time when small rural communities had a strong sense of communal identity and pride. In the Ashville area, the physical manifestations of this sense of belonging can be found in communal directories that listed every single person and a quilt that listed everyone sewn in cursive.

Don Hatfield of South Bloomfield is just one of hundreds of innovators and patented inventors from the Ashville area.

Chapter Four

Decades Ahead of Their Time

Ohio inventors are credited with producing a large number of game-changing innovations, including the light bulb, phonograph, motion picture camera, internal combustion automobile, electric automobile, rubber, cash register, airplane, and the pop-top soda can. That's a pretty impressive list.

Inventors from the Ashville area have also made their mark. Sometimes they were a commercial success and sometimes they merely inspired further innovations by others—years after their patents were issued.

One local inventor's device was so futuristic that it stopped traffic and entered *Guinness World Records*. The demonstration of another invention brought out the curious who worried the inventor would plunge to his death—he didn't. Ashville is also proud that it had one of the first multi-patented women inventors.

Stopping Traffic

Ashville's traffic light was such an attraction that from the 1930s through the 1970s people from across Ohio would drive to town just to watch it do what it was supposed to do—direct traffic at the intersection of Main and Long Streets. The patented invention of Theodore Boor stood the test of time and found its way into *Guinness World Records* as the oldest continuously operating traffic signal.

Theodore Boor and his original traffic light in 1940.

The light has a single lens that faces the driver and a sweeping hand much like a second hand on a watch that informs drivers how much time they must wait until it is their turn to go. The lens changes colors from red to green and from green to red when the second hand makes its revolution.

It is a celebrity of sorts, if that is possible for a mechanical device. It has appeared on the *Oprah Winfrey Show* and *An American Moment, with James Earl Jones*. Boor's light has also been featured in hundreds of travel and curiosity publications over the years.

It has been said that there never was a traffic accident at that light, even though there was a good chance if you were colorblind you might not be able to tell if the light was green or red. Perhaps locals were so wary of drivers running that light that they were overly cautious at that intersection.

The pride of Ashville was taken down in the 1970s because it did not meet the State of Ohio requirements that standardized all traffic signals. However, one can still witness it changing colors at the entrance of the museum.

Not the first traffic light.

Local residents often credit Teddy Boor with inventing the world's first traffic light in 1932. In Ohio, people credit an African American named Garrett Morgan with inventing the first traffic light. The truth is that neither of these wonderful gentlemen invented the traffic light.

James Hoge from Cleveland is credited with patenting the "first electric traffic signal." His design was installed on August 5, 1914. William Ghiglieri of San Francisco was the first to patent an automatic traffic signal that used red and green lights. His patent was issued in 1917.

Morgan, who was also from Cleveland, patented his traffic signal in 1923. It was not a traffic light, but it was the first to develop a system that gave drivers time to stop in all directions before signaling that one direction could go. Morgan also invented the gas mask.

Boor's light was the first motorized traffic light, and it still holds the record as the longest-operating traffic signal in the world. Boor's invention was not the only traffic light patented by a local inventor. Charles Clark of Orient, Ohio, patented his traffic signal in 1943. Like Boor's unique device, Clark's signal provided motorists an idea of how long they would be waiting before the signal changed.

I Will Sign My Own Name

Eliza M. (Fridley) Steward of Ashville is one of only a handful of nineteenth-century women to have filed for and received multiple patents. During this period of our nation, even if a woman created an idea, she would be advised to have her husband file the patent.

When you consider that only thirty-two women had

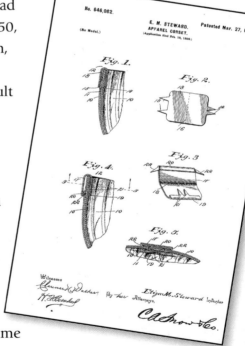

been issued patents by the year 1850, compared to ten thousand for men, you have to wonder why. For one thing, property laws made it difficult for women to acquire patents— they could not own property, but their husbands could. Even when women gained property rights, many of those women signed with only their initials to hide the fact that they were female. They did so to escape ridicule.

Not Eliza M. Steward. She did not file under her husband's name. She boldly displayed her name as the female inventor on both of her patents.

Today, local women inventors like Anita Waggy, Dawn Peterson, Ivowen Triplett, and Chrystal Gillilan are adding their names to a growing list.

Eliza Steward wasn't the only woman from this area to challenge traditional perceptions about the role of women. Florence Brobeck was one of the first women to develop a national magazine. Vivian (Runkle) Michael was a puppetry innovator. Gale Warner was an important environmental activist. Diana Blaney is among the first female scientists to manage a space mission. Corinne (Welsh) Morgan was an important early recording artist. Sarah Fisher wasn't just the first female owner of an IRL team to win an event—she was also on the National Women's Business Council, an advisory panel to the president.

Nikki (Rush) Tinsley was the first woman named the Inspector General of the US Environmental Protection Agency. Attorney and judge Judith (Bowers) Nicely was one of the first women to present a case to the Ohio Supreme Court. Reverend Mary (Hinkle) Shore was appointed rector and dean of the Lutheran Theological Southern Seminary. Gretchen Anne Hedges Srigley Seitsinger was one of the first female hospital administrators in America, serving at the Newark Methodist Maternity Hospital in El Paso, Texas.

All of these women had other local female role models that held leadership positions in business, town government, civic associations, political organizations, and lodge activities.

Diana Blaney (far left kneeling), Women in Science photo with Mars rover.
Courtesy NASA

Poo-Powered Batteries

Being the first or youngest to do something of note is worthy. Eliza Steward was the first female patented inventor from the area and Ross Larue is the youngest by far.

In 1994 Ross Larue—a student scientist at Teays Valley High School—patented his sewage sludge compost battery. Before you get all grossed out, please note that there is a big difference between treated sewage and sewage sludge compost.

Ross determined that naturally occurring aerobic and anaerobic bacteria found in sewage sludge compost could produce usable electrical current, and that current could be enhanced with the addition of compounds that included nitrogen—such as urea. Just as a regular battery's electrical current is produced when dissimilar electrodes (a cathode and an anode) are inserted into an electrolyte medium in a metal casing, the same could occur with the sludge compost and nitrogen mixture acting as an electrolyte medium.

You may think his idea odd, but really what he is suggesting is that biological oxidation and other reduction reactions that exist in the creation of sewage sludge compost are capable of producing electrical energy. By failing to capture this energy source, are we wasting waste?

Everybody has to start somewhere.

Sewage sludge batteries may have been a small sign that Ross Larue was destined to develop a career in biochemistry. Today Dr. Larue's research interests include:

Identifying novel interactions between host and virally encoded proteins, elucidating the role of cellular cofactors in guiding integration site selection of retroviral integrases, discerning structural determinates for interactions between host proteins, retroviral integrases and select chromatin marks, and investigating methods to improve gammaretroviral based vectors for human gene-therapy.

Dr. Ross Larue Courtesy Ohio State University

Look Away, He's Gonna Jump!

Samuel Preston Deeds had an unusual idea in 1895. After reading about the loss of life from numerous wooden hotel fires, he designed a portable fire escape that looked a lot like a

common tape measure. It was six inches in diameter and weighed only five pounds. It had one hundred and fifty feet of steel ribbon rated to withstand one thousand pounds of breaking strain.

In the event of a fire, the lucky owner could just attach the device to a bedpost or anything else that would anchor it in the room, climb into or grab the loops attached to the machine, and lower him- or herself to the ground.

Mr. Deeds was the secretary of the Scioto Valley Canning Factory in 1907, and since that was the tallest occupied structure in Ashville, he decided he would demonstrate his newly patented device from the third floor. Hundreds of workers and townspeople came to watch Deeds cast himself to the ground below. He climbed out of the window and to the anguish, and then delight, of all those present, he gently descended to the ground. He was roundly praised by the onlookers.

Deeds built a local factory in Ashville to manufacture his patented device, but he was unable to generate the sales needed to support its production. On the positive side, his patent has been cited by other patents that built upon his idea to provide external fire escape mechanisms that would enable people to safely exit high-rise buildings.

Filter out any distractions.

Sam Deeds was not able to successfully market his idea, but in 1965 Harold Pontius was able to do exactly that. He focused on manufacturing range hood filters and turning his vision into a thriving business. Columbus Industries today is a global company that designs, manufactures, and markets a wide range of air filter products.

The company he started has expertise in the design and use of metal filters, charcoal filters, high-efficiency filters, paper paint collectors, humidifier pads, aquarium filters, and furnace filters. Harold and his son Jeff also hold numerous patents on filtering media for range hoods, humidifiers, and capturing odors.

Columbus Industries founder Harold T. Pontius. Courtesy Columbus Industries

At the present time, Columbus Industries has over nine hundred associates in seven locations worldwide. The headquarters is located in Ashville.

What Is the Capital of Bolivia?

Long before the game Trivial Pursuit or the game show *Jeopardy* became sensations, Don Hatfield of South Bloomfield developed a brain game that tested one's knowledge about a variety of subjects. He created a tabletop device he called Eye Cue that was designed to entertain restaurant patrons while they waited for their food to be prepared.

The Eye Cue device stood only about five inches tall and was freestanding. For a penny, you and your tablemates would be presented with a new question that appeared in a small window, followed by the answer. You did not win anything if you got the answer right—just the satisfaction that you were endowed with a great deal of useless knowledge.

Don's children Lorna and David scoured through encyclopedias, newspapers, and almanacs to find appropriate questions and answers. They assembled them on a paper roll that could be scrolled.

The restaurant owner could purchase different question-and-answer rolls to be inserted in the Eye Cue. Each roll contained 150 questions and answers. Don's idea was tested locally, but it did not catch on. The concept he developed was later proven to be a draw with some sports-themed restaurants that allowed patrons to use electronic devices to select their answers to questions that appeared on a screen. By the way, Sucre is the official and judicial capital of Bolivia, while La Paz is the seat of the executive and legislative branches of the national government—TRICK QUESTION.

Higher education.

There has never been a college or university in the Ashville area, but that does not mean that local people look down on higher education. It is true that Otterbein College started at a United Brethren church meeting in Walnut Township. It is also true that Ashville had a "normal" school above the Ashville Bank that prepared high school graduates to pass a teaching exam, but it never developed beyond that.

One family that would certainly get high marks for its commitment to education would be that of George and Clara Bowers of Walnut Township. They had four children—Harold, Helen, Stanley, and Georgia. George was a farmer, educator, and state representative, but he died of a brain tumor when he was forty-five years old. Harold, the oldest, was just twelve when his father died, and Georgia was born six weeks after her father's death.

While Clara placed a high value on education, she expected Harold to take over the farm. Harold convinced his mother that he should give college a try and leave the farming to a tenant. He took on a wide variety of summer jobs to pay for his room and board—even digging ditches. He graduated from Ohio Northern University with a bachelor of science in education. He proved himself to be a great teacher and an excellent administrator at the local level.

Just ten years after he graduated, he was recruited by the state Department of Education, where he achieved a national reputation in the field of teacher certification. When he retired, he was Deputy Superintendent of Public Instruction for the state. His son, Dr. G. Robert Bowers was Ohio's Assistant Superintendent of Public Instruction for a record tenure of nineteen years.

Harold's sisters, Helen and Georgia, graduated from college as teachers. Both Helen and Harold had masters degrees. His brother, Stanley, obtained a law degree and made a name for himself as Ohio's tax commissioner. Not a bad family legacy.

Driverless Car

The prospect of self-driving cars is no longer a distant dream for automotive engineers, but in 1964 the thought of a driverless car would be frightening. In 1964 and 1965 several miles of public roadway adjacent to the town of Ashville were used to test an automated car that did not need a driver.

The technical wizards behind this automated highway vehicle designed a car that had a sensor that guided the car by following an electromagnetic field emitted by two parallel wires attached to the pavement. The car seemed to work quite well, and there were no accidents or incidents in which the car was out of control.

This was the first public roadway test of the automated highway. The tests were so successful that newspapers and magazines from around the world did stories about something that was unthinkable, if not downright scary—a car that could never respond to a backseat driver.

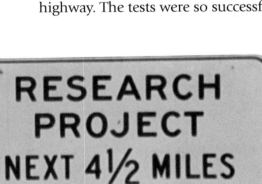

Sign on Circleville Lockbourne Eastern. Courtesy Earl Boyer collection

Ashville area patent material

On every street and down every country road.

It may seem trite or overly pompous to say this, but you can go down any street or road in the Ashville area and you will find the home of a patented inventor, entertainer, graphic artist, recording artist, or a published author. It is true that not all of these creative individuals have achieved national recognition, but it does say something about rural small towns being undervalued incubators of creativity.

There is a map at the end of this book that provides a glimpse of where some of the hundreds of patented inventors, published authors, movie actors, sports figures, heroes, entertainers, recording artists, graphic artists, scientists, politicians, and other notable persons once lived. The density of accomplished people tied to Ashville, Commercial Point, Orient, and South Bloomfield made it impossible to show them all on this map. You can pick up a map of each community illustrating that at the museum.

On Paper, It Will Fly

In 1910 the *New York Times* ran a story about local area inventor John Oman's quest to build a gyroplane that would carry up to one hundred passengers. They called his patented invention the realization of Jules Verne's fanciful 1865 novel, *From the Earth to the Moon.* In fact, illustrations of a large airship racing across the face of the moon adorn the stock certificates of the Universal

Oman Aircraft stock certificate

Aerial Navigation Company that Oman founded in St. Louis to build his fantastical invention.

Stories about Oman's airship ran in newspapers across America in a shrewd attempt to market the company's stock. There was just one problem. Although the small patented model of Oman's plane would fly, when the full-sized metal frame version was built, it could not get off the ground. The enormous engines required to lift the weight of the airship and the pilot had not been developed. Oman tried to get around that problem by inventing a compressed air motor, which he patented to drive the propellers on his craft.

It still would not budge. So, his bravado in openly challenging the Wright Brothers to be the first to build a commercial carrier to transport the masses fell flat. However, you could fold a stock certificate into a paper airplane and it would fly.

Oman grew up on a farm that is now part of the Slate Run Metro Park. His homestead has been preserved as it would have been when he was a boy.

Sifting moon dust.

The moon may have been a futuristic travel destination for Jules Verne and John Oman, but a local inventor, Charles Ward, played an important role in America's most important space adventure—the Apollo 11 moon landing. Charles was a vibration and sound technician in Allen-Bradley's Special Machine Department in Milwaukee. It was there in 1958 that he developed a sifter

Apollo 11 moon dust.
Courtesy NASA

that used sound waves to screen or sieve industrial powders. Mechanical sifters were in use prior to this time, but they often destroyed the original size of the particles, so Ward's invention was a big advancement.

The Allen-Bradley Company was rightly proud that Ward's sonic sifter was used by NASA to "sift the secrets of the moon." Astronauts Neil Armstrong and Buzz Aldrin collected rock samples and lunar soil and subsoil. When they returned to earth, the soil samples were immediately run through the sonic sifter. Scientists at the Lunar Receiving Lab identified the sample material as volcanically produced rock. Additional analyses found unexpectedly large amounts of titanium, chromium, zirconium, and yttrium, but no indication of water or organic material.

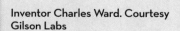

Inventor Charles Ward. Courtesy Gilson Labs

Murder-for-Hire model from Ashville caused a run on the dress design she wore at her trial. It sold out nationwide.

Chapter Five

Not Normal

There are just some human actions that are so outside the bounds of normative behavior that we are compelled to marvel at the bad choices people have made (recognizing not all bad choices were deliberate). Ohio's gallery of notoriously bad actors who once lived in the state includes Charles Manson, John Holmes, Jeffery Dahmer, Ariel Castro, and John Dillinger. John Holmes was born in the Ashville area and Ariel Castro died there.

Another candidate for Ohio's list is Earl Ellery Wright, who made the FBI's Ten Most Wanted list after robbing the Ashville Bank. National outrage followed the vigilante lynching of Tom McDonald near Commercial Point, so that also merits consideration. The area even managed to capture the international spotlight with several bizarre cases involving murder, attempted murder, robbery, and child custody.

One could argue that this type of notoriety is generally not wanted. There is, however, sort of a perverse pride in having Dwight Yoakam claim the "rowdiest bar he ever played in" was here.

Occupation: Outlaw

When your occupation listed in the US Census is "outlaw," you might not be overly surprised when a bunch of masked men break into your house with guns drawn carrying a rope. You have to think something bad is about to happen. It is probably why Tom McDonald asked, "Are you boys gonna kill me?"

The lynching of Tom McDonald that happened on Anne Dechert's farm near Commercial Point was a seminal event that drew condemnation from local and national press. Essentially, McDonald was known for being belligerent to the townspeople living in Commercial Point. He got into a fight with store owner Martin Beavers (a cousin related to his wife) in which Beavers got the better of him (nearly removing his only eye). McDonald threatened to get even.

Tom McDonald's unmarked grave is in the Presbyterian Cemetery.

Several days later, near the midnight hour, eight to ten men converged on the McDonald homestead, where he was still convalescing. They entered his room with guns drawn and tied a noose around his neck in front of his wife, Alice. Then they drug him in the dark thousands of feet across the road to a wooded area next to the road adjacent to his mother-in-law's farm.

The dragging was so brutal that it almost tore a nipple off his chest. There they strung him up with a note attached to his nearly naked body warning that anyone who tried to threaten similar violence would meet the same fate. No one was ever charged with the murder of Tom McDonald. His body was removed the next morning and placed on display, then buried later that same day in an unmarked grave at the Commercial Point Presbyterian Church's cemetery.

Hanging at Main and Long.

On November 11, 1918, from early in the morning until noon, every church bell, factory whistle, and the school bell in Ashville rang continuously without stopping to signal that World War I had ended. A little before two o'clock in the afternoon, people armed with flags descended upon the ritualized hanging of Kaiser Wilhelm's effigy at the intersection of Main and Long to start a parade. Here is Steve Fridley's description:

The Kaiser (paddy) had been hung in the middle of the street at the intersection of Main and Long Streets during the morning and here it was that the afternoon parade formed for march.

The hearse was drawn to the scene by two mules and the carcass was lowered and a coffin was taken from the hearse and the body roughly put in the casket and "gently" pressed down by the feet of the honorary pall bearers, who then placed the casket into the conveyance and the parade was on. The procession was more or less a mile long, composed of humanity and decorated automobiles.

The principal streets were made in the march and procession finally rounded into the school grounds where the Kaiser was taken from the hearse and cremated in the presence of the many assembled.

Nobody's Perfect, Your Honor

Earl Ellery Wright staked out and robbed the Ashville Bank on November 17, 1966. He held a gun on the employees, forcing the manager to tape and tie them all up and lock them in the bank vault. The thirty-six-year-old Wright escaped with almost $50,000. Six months before, he had held up the tellers at the Suburban Trust Company in Coral Hills, Maryland. He netted $61,000 in that job.

The increasing frequency of his robberies and the increasingly threatening manner in which he conducted them caused the FBI to place him on their Ten Most Wanted list. He was eventually arrested and spent almost a decade in federal prison. After he was released, he returned to a life of crime. In 1979 he robbed a BancOhio branch in Berea, then several months later hit another BancOhio branch in North Olmsted. The job in North Olmsted became a hostage situation that ultimately resulted in the release of the hostages and his capture.

Judge Robert Krupansky noted at Wright's sentencing that the defendant had led a long life of crime, committing robberies, forgeries, and kidnapping. The judge asked if Mr. Wright or his attorney wanted to make a statement before he pronounced the sentence. Wright's lawyer stood up and said, "Nobody's Perfect, Your Honor."

A match cover did him in.

The Ashville Bank had been robbed and the FBI was on the scene looking for clues. Town marshal, Glenn Clay, proved to have the most important evidence that might lead to the person responsible for terrorizing bank employees and walking off with more than $50,000.

Orlan Hines reported days earlier that a suspicious person was following two of his sons in a car as they made their early morning paper deliveries. Hines was an executive vice president at the Ashville Bank. After the boys got home from their routes, the car was parked across the street from the Hines residence, and Mr. Hines was able to identify a license plate number using one of his children's telescopes.

Hines told Marshal Clay about the suspicious car and gave him the license plate number. Clay promptly wrote the number of the back of a match cover. He had the match cover with him when he entered the bank after the robbery. He had a strong suspicion that the person following the Hines boys was also the bank robber.

Marshal Glenn Clay
Courtesy *Columbus Dispatch*

Clay provided the FBI with his match cover information, and within an hour they knew the driver was—Earl Ellery Wright. They figured he would be looking to buy a new car before taking off from the Columbus area. They were right. He was found at a Columbus car dealership, but Wright artfully escaped the agents waiting outside the dealership bathroom for him.

Perfect Attendance

There is no delicate way to approach the subject of a notorious adult film star from Millport—John Curtis Estes Holmes. He was born August 8, 1944. When he was delivered by Dr. Ralph Hosler of Ashville, Hosler purportedly was initially worried that the boy was born with a third leg. John was a normal kid. He loved to go hunting and exploring along Little Walnut Creek and the canal, riding his bike and playing with friends. He had a lifelong obsession with nature and worked to preserve the natural world.

He loved visiting with his grandparents John and Bessie—who lived on Jefferson Avenue in Ashville. His mother was a devout Southern Baptist who saw to it that her children regularly attended church and Sunday school in Millport, even though the family had moved to Columbus when John was seven. Years later, when John was being tried as an accomplice to the Wonderland, California, murders, it was noted in his defense that he had fifteen years of perfect Sunday school attendance in the Millport Baptist Church.

John's life and times are well documented elsewhere. He was known worldwide as the "King of Porn," and was a poster boy for America's AIDS epidemic. He was given an AIDS diagnosis in 1985 and had slowly withered away to just ninety pounds by the time he died in 1988.

You might think that delivering John Holmes might be the most memorable event in this country doctor's career. Far from it. One of Dr. Hosler's memorable moments occurred in 1928, when he was cast in a silent film as a physician who saved the life of inventor Teddy Boor. In the film, Boor was attacked by workers who were going to be displaced by his new labor-saving farm machinery.

The farm laborers attacked Boor and attempted to burn both him and his invention. Boor was pulled from the burning heap as Hosler raced to the scene to provide emergency aid. In time, Hosler nurtured him back to good health. Local inventor Audrey Graham played the chief antagonist as the leader of the disgruntled workers.

Starring in a silent film was interesting, but that was not the crowning achievement of his life. Many local people would argue that he saved many lives. He truly was a blessing to the community. But that is not all he did for the community. When he died in 1978, he left much of his sizeable estate to the Hosler Foundation to finance medical scholarships for graduates of the Teays Valley and Amanda-Clearcreek School Districts.

As a result, there are more medical practitioners from the area, per student population, than almost any comparable area in the state. The Hosler program also funds the Teays Valley and Amanda-Clearcreek Science Study Enrichment Programs, which focus on improving math and science study skills.

C'mon Now, We Have All Done Something Stupid

In the category of "you just cannot make this stuff up," the *London Daily Mail* designated the robber of the Ashville Savings Bank and his girlfriend as the "dumbest thieves ever" after they posed for Facebook with the thousands of dollars of cash

stolen from the bank. As the *Daily Mail* noted, the robber had just been released from prison one month earlier for a separate robbery, when "he walked into the bank wearing a black hoodie that covered his rather distinctive facial tattoos—he has 'Loyalty's Thin' on his right cheek and 'Betrayal's Thick' on his left—and handed the teller a note."

One week later, the robber posted a selfie to his Facebook page showing a wad of cash in his mouth. Then he posted two other photos with the stolen money, including one with his girlfriend.

It wasn't long after those postings that authorities started receiving tips about the pair. One of the photos showed the couple posing beside a State of Georgia sign that was on the wall of a rest stop—kind of a clue as to their potential whereabouts.

Not many of us do something this smart.

Big things are expected of you when you graduate from the Massachusetts Institute of Technology (MIT) in electrical engineering. Richard Valentine Baum was up to the challenge.

Richard was born on April 19, 1925, to Clarence and Hattie (Valentine) Baum in Ashville. His parents moved to Corpus Christi, Texas, when he was just a boy. As a teenager he built his own radios and was an avid ham radio operator. He had a high IQ and was easily accepted into MIT.

After graduation in 1948, he went to work for Goodyear Aerospace in Akron, then transferred to Arizona, where he collaborated with other electronics wizards to develop a Doppler unbeamed search radar. Baum holds seven patents related to radar, including the simultaneous buildup Doppler radar.

He was considered a leader in the field of radar systems for planes and ships. When he retired, he was the Manager of Divisional Engineering at Goodyear Aerospace.

DC-3 cockpit with a Goodyear Aerospace radar system

Wait a Minute, What?

It was a national story on surrogate birth so bizarre that it would have stymied Maury Povich. A local woman shot and killed the father of their child after an acrimonious custody dispute. He was coming to pick up the child, having won custody earlier in the day. She said that she shot him because he assaulted her upon entering her apartment.

The child was born to a surrogate paid by the mother and father to bear his child. But the child of the surrogate was not fathered by the father. Here is the full confusing story as the *New York Times* reported it:

> *The story of Beverly Seymour, Richard Reams and their child may be one of the most convoluted surrogacy cases ever, beginning when Ms. Seymour and Mr. Reams discovered that they could not have children of their own and entered into a surrogacy contract with Norma Lee Stotski, paying her $10,000 to bear them a child through artificial insemination with Mr. Reams's sperm.*
>
> *But the contract expired without a pregnancy. Later, Ms. Stotski told Ms. Seymour that she was pregnant and offered Ms. Seymour the baby. Ms. Seymour and Mr. Reams took the day-old baby girl in January 1985. And although the original birth certificate showed Ms. Stotski's husband as the father, it was changed to name Mr. Reams.*
>
> *Ms. Seymour and Mr. Reams divorced the next year. In the ensuing fight for custody, Ms. Seymour sought and won blood tests showing that the biological father was neither Mr. Reams nor Ms. Stotski's husband, but a third man.*

The end of polygamy.

Although almost all Christian bioethicists argue that surrogacy violates the "creation norm for marriage, family, and procreation, by introducing a third-party contributor," it pales in comparison as a political issue to the hue and cry against polygamy as practiced by the Mormon Church in the late 1800s.

George Peters was born here on October 11, 1846. After graduation he taught school locally, but he decided to turn his attention to the legal profession and moved to Columbus. In 1881 he was elected mayor of the city of Columbus.

In 1887 after leaving the office of mayor, Peters was appointed by President Grover Cleveland to become the United States Attorney for the Utah Territory. He willingly stepped into a hornets' nest. It was his task to disincorporate the LDS Church and the Perpetual Emigration Fund on the grounds that they fostered polygamy. It fell upon Peters's shoulders to prosecute the church and seize church property. The first piece of property seized was the Tithing Office. Next the Gardo House and Historian's Office were taken, and then the Temple Block. All were rented back to the church for a yearly fee. Work on the Salt Lake Temple ceased after these proceedings.

The Mormon Church supported marriage to multiple wives.

Peters's actions had the desired effect—on September 25, 1890, the head of the church, Wilford Woodruff, issued a manifesto whereby he made it known that God spoke to him and the church. They were called to submit to the laws of Congress, which prohibited the practice of polygamy.

Don't Drink the Water

You can be certain that in 1914, when former Ashville resident Dr. Harley M. Plum earned acclaim for his chemical reduction of carnotite ore into its radioactive constituents, he was advancing the cause of science. Indeed, he was hired by Standard Chemical in Pittsburgh as one of only fifteen staff that were producing high-grade radium in the United States at their Oakland, Pennsylvania, laboratory. Plum's process was used to refine

Dr. Harley M. Plum

radium and vanadium salts from the carnotite ore at Standard Chemical's reduction mill in Canonsburg, Pennsylvania.

One of the highlights of his time with Standard Chemical happened on May 26 and 27, 1921, when Madame Curie was an honored guest at the Canonsburg and Oakland facilities. She came to the United States to receive a small amount of radium for her research.

At the time, radium was being used as a treatment for cancer, but it was unfortunate that scientists did not yet understand how dangerous repeated exposure to it was for those working with it, ingesting it, and transporting it. Many health experts at the time thought that a little bit of radium in the water

Madame Curie at Standard Chemical in Pittsburgh. Courtesy Harley Plum Collection

could restore a person's health—claiming that it could reduce high blood pressure and relieve arthritis. Standard Chemical advertised radium salts for drinking water and bath water and for injections and compresses. They recommended drinking the solution daily, during or after meals.

Perhaps it would have been better if the company's products were more like snake oil, with fraudulent claims that it contained radium. Unfortunately, they did contain radium, and many people who sought radium cures or relief ended up getting stomach cancers and dying. Then there is the sad case of young women who were hired to paint radium on watch dials who died from throat and mouth cancers induced because they licked their brushes before dipping them into radium paint.

High-level nuclear waste.

In the 1980s the US Department of Energy asked Battelle Memorial Institute in Columbus to write a handbook of community development for communities that could potentially host the nation's first high-level nuclear waste repository. The report was to make impacted communities aware of the kinds of federal assistance that would be made available to them—especially programs to address the possible influx of workers. There would be demands on their infrastructure, schools, and social services.

The potential sites in Texas, Utah, Mississippi, and Louisiana were rural in nature, so in order to illustrate the handbook, Battelle looked for a nearby rural community. They chose Ashville. Photographs of buildings and people from Ashville appeared in their book.

Liquid Poison

An early history of Walnut Township noted that the township seemed to have developed a special fondness for turning its crops into distilled spirits. While one could argue that shipping whiskey was a more efficient way to move the farmer's product, nevertheless, the newspaper's editor scolded them thusly:

It [Walnut Township] has a large proportion of good corn land, and produces abundant crops of wheat, oats, rye, and grass. There are more distilleries of whisky in this township than in all the rest of the county; and it is to be regretted that the inhabitants have not seen it more for their interest, to convert their large surplus of corn and rye into pork and beef, than into this "liquid poison."

The advent of the Ohio and Erie Canal in nearby Millport made it easier to ship bulk grains to markets starting in the 1830s, but Walnut Township held onto its cottage industry. It was disconcerting to some residents of the township that there were more distilleries than churches. However, by the 1870s most of these small distilleries were abandoned.

National Liquor Company.

In the 1830s Richard Stiage started a grist mill and distillery along Walnut Creek that was purchased in the late 1830s by Mahlon and Absalom Ashbrook. They made a go of it for a while, but by 1855 they had gone bankrupt. Undeterred by the failure of that earlier venture, Mr. Collins and Mr. Stone established the National Liquor Company in the town of Ashville in 1907.

Sixty years later, Bill Welsh was exploring the old town dump when he came across a bottle from the short-lived National Liquor Company. Today, that bottle resides in Ohio's Small Town Museum. The bottle advertised that they offered whiskey, cordial alcohol, brandy, gin, and compound wine.

Now a person can get a bite to eat and drink spirits at Ashbrook Distillery and Grill at 22 Long Street. Although there is no distillery that is run by this restaurant, they do have a selection of liquors that would make the original distillery owners green with envy.

This business operates out of the same building that once housed Clyde Brinker's restaurant. It was the home of Buster—the Dog that voted Republican—and the diner of choice for Chic-Chic—the world's smartest rooster. It has a lot of old-time area photos from bygone eras posted on its walls.

The Rowdiest Bar in America?

Country music legend Dwight Yoakam played in a lot of honky-tonk bars in his time—including the famous Blackboard in Bakersfield, California. But out of the hundreds of bars in which he played, there was only one he deemed "the roughest bar I ever played in." That title goes to the Stagecoach Inn in

South Bloomfield. Yoakam grew up in Columbus and did some gigs in the area before he moved to California to seek fame and fortune. But his gig at the iconic Stagecoach Inn left a lasting impression. It is hard to do a set of older songs when the crowd wants you to only do new cover songs. It is hard to play when people are punching it out in front of the stage.

While the young Yoakam did not have the best reception at the inn, many other local acts were able to hone their skills playing for the patrons there. The inn also had a softer side when it came to food. People in the area loved their outstanding barbeque fare, but unfortunately the inn succumbed to a fire in April of 2008. It was a total loss.

Dwight had two number-one country singles during his fabulous career, but there is someone from this area that managed to have three national number-one recordings. Corinne Morgan (February 16, 1876– March 23, 1942) was the stage name of Corinne Welsh. The contralto was a pioneering recording artist who hit the charts with popular songs in the early years of the twentieth century. She had a solo career but was best known for her duets with Frank Stanley.

She was born in Commercial Point, Ohio, the daughter of John C. Welsh and Rachel Welsh, and later moved to New York City. In 1902 she started recording for the major cylinder recording companies of the day, although after 1904 most of her recordings were for Victor Records. She was one of the first female singers to record regularly, and she mainly recorded sentimental songs. Her number-one records were "Listen to the Mocking Bird" (1904), "Toyland" (1904), and "So Long, Mary" (1906). She recorded more than one hundred cylinders and flat records during her career.

Contralto singers usually have a heavier tone and more power than other female singers. They are rare indeed. Morgan helped pave the way for modern pop contralto recording stars like Cher, Karen Carpenter, and Grace Slick.

Morgan was also not the only recording artist to hail from this area. King Records pressed several songs featuring fingerpicking guitarist Al Myers bopping with the Country Cats and the Georgia Crackers. Capitol Records contracted with Dr. Ellis Snyder's Capital University Chapel Choir to produce choral music. Atlantic Records had a contract with the country rock group McGuffey Lane.

James "Buster" Douglas appears in *The Wager*—a movie starring Ashville actor/writer/producer Jim Gloyd.

STARRING:

JIM
GLOYD

CAMERON
ARNETT

BISHOP
STEVENS

TY
SHELTON

JOHN
WELLS

JAMES BUSTER
DOUGLAS

ANDIE
STANEK

THE WAGER

JIMMY RAY GLOYD PRESENTS A CLEANSCREEN PRODUCTION "THE WAGER"

DIRECTED BY MARK JUSTICE   PRODUCED BY JIMMY RAY GLOYD   ASSISTANT DIRECTOR RICHIE JOHNS   EXECUTIVE PRODUCER DAMIIAN TANENBAUM

MUSIC BY COLE TAGUE   AMANDA BLANKENSHIP   DIRECTOR OF PHOTOGRAPHY VINCENT MCVAY   PRODUCTION DESIGNER DOUG WHITLATCH

COMING SOON

WWW.THEWAGERMOVIE.COM

Chapter Six

Unexpected Outcomes

No one in Ohio or anywhere else expected Buster Douglas to knock out Mike Tyson for the heavyweight title. Few expected Harry Truman to win the presidential election against Thomas Dewey.

When it comes to delivering unexpected outcomes, Ashville is in a class by itself. No one in their right mind would expect three prominent naval commanders and two internationally respected oceanographers to come from a landlocked community like Ashville. No one would have ever expected to find buried silver nuggets, or ancient parallel and right-angle pits there.

Ashville is also replete with stories that should not be plausible and stories where the intended or observed outcomes failed miserably. These are stories that made people question their judgment after the fact but are the source of good-natured ribbings today.

Silver Surprise

In 1897 the Ohio State Archaeological and Historical Society sent Dr. Clarence Loveberry to Ashville to meet with the owner of an upland mound group known as the Snake Den. It was so named because snakes actually denned up in the mounds over the winter and emerged every spring.

Loveberry came armed with a letter from Governor Bushnell, seeking permission to conduct a field study at the site. He presented it to the owner, a farmer and local politician named Dildine Snyder. Snyder looked over the letter and agreed to allow the investigation under one condition—if any gold or silver was found, it belonged to him and he had the right to shut down the fieldwork.

Loveberry was aware that no silver had been found in any upland mounds in Ohio and was quite comfortable with the owner's stipulation. Work began on the site with several unremarkable burials being found in a clay mound. But a few days into the study, the workers ran into something quite remarkable. They found a large cache of geologic and man-made material in the center platform above a stone sarcophagus-like box that contained cremated remains. Just above the stone lid of that box they found a container of silver nuggets.

Loveberry took the nuggets to Columbus, where they were verified as silver. When he got back to the site, Snyder informed him that he wanted the nuggets and all the digging had to stop.

Loveberry pleaded with him to donate them for science and begged for extra time. In the end, Loveberry bought the nuggets for many times more than they were worth and was allowed two more days to wrap up the field study.

The nuggets and their container became an attraction at the newly formed Ohio State Archaeological and Historical Society Museum in Columbus. They also represented Ohio, along with other artifacts from mound builders, at both the Louisiana Purchase Exposition in St. Louis and the Jamestown Exposition in Jamestown, Virginia.

Search for missing silver nuggets.

All of the geologic and man-made items taken from the Snake Den mounds fieldwork in 1897 were cataloged and retained by the Ohio State Archaeological and Historical Society. Some things, like the snake bones and silver nuggets with their container, were oddities of interest to the general public.

Over time, some items became separated from the collection. At one point, curators for the society were unable to locate *any* items from the Snake Den Collection. Current-day archaeological curators from Ohio History Connection (formerly the Ohio State Archaeological and Historical Society), using modern search techniques and informed hunches, have been able to reassemble part of this material. They have been able to locate many of the items, but four of the original five silver nuggets have yet to be located. So, the search goes on.

Landlocked Naval Commanders

Commander Rexford Arnett Jr. with Commander Rodney Kauber in New York

The closest body of water to Ashville, Ohio, is Stage's Pond—a small thirty-acre kettle lake. Hardly the place to launch a naval career, but that little town has produced three naval commanders—Harley Hannibal Christy, Richard S. Hudson, and Rodney K. Kauber. Christy actually rose to become a Vice Admiral. Hudson was in charge of naval supplies and logistics at Subic Bay in the Philippines during the Vietnam War and was awarded the Navy Commendation Medal. Commander Kauber was a pilot and squadron leader.

Commander Richard Hudson receiving the Navy Commendation Medal

Of the three, Christy arguably had the most eventful career. In World War I, he commanded the USS *San Diego*. On the morning of July 19, 1918, that ship hit a German mine off the coast of Long Island, New York. The ship was doomed. She started to list and capsize and sank less than half an hour after she was hit. The crew was well drilled for such an event, and when the captain gave the signal to abandon ship, nearly all the seamen were saved—only six perished in the explosion and its aftermath. In the finest traditions of the sea, Christy was the last to depart from the ship.

Admiral H. H. Christy

Christy was hailed as a hero by the *New York Times* and was awarded the Distinguished Service Medal for his service during that war.

Landlocked oceanographers.

It is crazy that three naval commanders came from the small landlocked farming village of Ashville, but it is downright irrational to believe that two important American oceanographers also came from this area. Still, it is true.

Oceanographer
Steven K. Baum

Look in Wikipedia under "Oceanography" and you will find that oceanographer Steven K. Baum, who grew up in Duvall, is responsible for the often-cited *Glossary of Physical Oceanography and Related Disciplines*. Dr. Baum works out of Texas A&M in the Department of Oceanography.

You will also discover that the Henry Stommel Research Medal is granted each year by the American Meteorological Society to a person who has made outstanding contributions to the advancement of the understanding of the dynamics and physics of the ocean. This is the highest award that the society can bestow upon an oceanographer.

Dr. Glenn Flierl, who grew up in Ashville, was presented this award in 2015 for his fundamental insights into the dynamics of vortices and geostrophic turbulence and their impact on marine ecosystems. Dr. Flierl was a professor at MIT and a graduate of Harvard.

Glenn Flierl with students

Newly built traction line station

Which Way Is North?

The town of Ashville eagerly awaited its new traction line station in 1905. It meant that commuters could more quickly reach other cities, from Portsmouth to Columbus, via this dedicated electrified rail line.

The masonry on the new structure that was to house a passenger waiting room and a small depot for goods being shipped in and out of town was beginning to take shape. It had reached the height of four feet when it was discovered that the passenger loading area and dock were on the wrong side of the building. The plan had been reversed—it should have been facing the third-rail tracks.

Not to be deterred, the masons quickly razed their work and started on a reverse version of the drawings they had been following. Someone simply did not convey which direction was north.

On the morning of December 16, 1919, Supreme Allied Commander General John J. "Black Jack" Pershing arrived at Camp Sherman by train from Dayton, Ohio. He and his staff were provided a hero's welcome at the station, where they met with General Glenn and Brigadier General Trent and their staffs. That night there was a reception with the citizens of Chillicothe, where he enjoyed a little dancing.

Pershing in Scioto Valley traction line car crossing Walnut Creek at Ashville

The next morning Pershing inspected Camp Sherman. Just after eleven o'clock he met with a reception committee from Columbus that was joining him in his ride to Columbus aboard a special Scioto Valley Traction Line car, Motor No. 117, with George Gallegher as motorman in his service uniform. The following is from General Pershing's diary:

Supreme Allied Commander General John "Black Jack" Pershing

> *Enroute we stopped for a few moments at Kingston [and] Circleville, where the mayor, Mr. J. J. Goeller, presented us with a bouquet of flowers on behalf of his fellow townsmen. We also stopped at Ashville. ... At each place I shook hands with a great many people and made a few remarks.*

A Token of My Love

Solomon Graumlich was a blacksmith and inventor who moved from East Ringgold to Duvall Station (known simply as Duvall today) around 1886. He had just patented his force feeder for a grain elevator when he married Isabella in 1888. To celebrate their love, he designed and built a two-story home in the shape of a heart, with each room like a chamber of a heart. They raised four of their children, Emmet, Matilda, George, and Ralph, in that home. It is also where he patented a band cutter and feeder for a threshing machine, an extension ladder firetruck, and a cultivator shovel.

Solomon Graumlich as a blacksmith in Duvall. Courtesy Pickaway County Genealogical Library

The advent of the automobile changed the demand for blacksmithing, so he moved his family to Circleville, where he became an automotive machinist. The heart-shaped home in Duvall has passed through several families, and the internal partitions have been modified over the years. The outside is essentially the same, except that an attachment has been added to the west. Still, the heart shape remains and can be seen from the front of the house.

Buckeye blacksmith.

Being a blacksmith seems to have provided Solomon Graumlich with the necessary skills to later become an auto mechanic. It was also an important skill that helped turn a South Bloomfield blacksmith into a political stump speaking star.

John W. Bear was indeed a blacksmith from South Bloomfield who accidentally became a high-profile speaker for the Whig Party during William Henry Harrison's presidential campaign in 1840. It all started when he showed up at a rally in Columbus still wearing part of his protective blacksmithing leather. One of his compatriots from South Bloomfield called for him to speak to the crowd. Being a natural born rabble-rouser, he roasted the anti-Whig newspaper editor and the crowd went wild.

The Whig leaders immediately knew they had something special and persuaded him to take his plainspoken blacksmithing political harangues on the road. In the years that followed, Bear stumped for other Whig presidential candidates, including John Tyler, Zachary Taylor, and Millard Fillmore. Abraham Lincoln was one of Bear's fellow stump speakers that he counted as a friend. Indeed, when Lincoln was assassinated, Bear was asked to give an impromptu eulogy to an assembly of shocked mourners in Pittsburgh:

MY FELLOW COUNTRYMEN: I have a word to say if you will listen to me for a moment. I have travelled all over this continent as well as many parts of other countries; I have been rich and I have been poor. I have been on the topmost ladder of fame and I have seen the valley below, but I must confess, that this is the darkest day of my life; our chieftain is slain and our nation mourns. I can say no more. My heart is too full for utterance. The best friend that this country ever had is this morning lying cold in the arms of death. God has permitted it to be so, therefore let us meekly bow to his will, for he doeth all things well.

Perplexing Parallel and Right-Angle Pits

Archaeologist Dr. Jarrod Burks surveyed the Snake Den site in 2007 using a magnetometer (an instrument that identifies magnetic disturbances in the soil—allowing archaeologists to see hidden features like fire pits and earthen enclosures that may have been covered over through the centuries and rendered unobservable by historic plowing). In the course of conducting this survey, Dr. Burks found that the site was much larger than earlier fieldwork had suggested. In fact, the site had a large outer enclosure earthwork that extended far beyond the three mounds that were identified as Snake Den.

There was also a small enclosure directly in line with the three mounds that was in the shape of a "squircle"—a square with rounded corners. The Hopewell culture commonly constructed these at their sacred sites. But the survey also discovered that there was a series of pits running in a parallel line from the center mound platform to beyond the outer enclosure. He also found a line of pits that are at a right angle to these pits. This type of pit design had not been identified in other mound-builder spaces.

These pits were a curiosity not only to Jarrod, but also to a team of archaeologists from Bloomsburg University and the State University of New York College at Geneseo. They excavated one of the pits and found some hickory charcoal that could be carbon dated. Based on the presence of a "squircle" and the burials at the mounds, the archaeologist thought that the site was probably a Hopewell location. However, the carbon dating of the pit indicated that it was used about 800 BC, well before the time of the Hopewell culture. This would seem to indicate that several cultures used this site.

So, the question is who built these pits and for what purpose? Were they fire pits or post holes?

Learning more about the daily lives of the ancient Hopewell.

Renewed national interest in the Hopewell culture has resulted in a number of recent archaeological field studies being conducted in the Ashville area. Two residential sites—one near the Scioto River on a farm in Harrison Township and one near the Snake Den Mounds Complex in Walnut Township—have hosted archaeologists from New York, Pennsylvania, and Ohio.

Anthropologists, archaeologists, paleoethnologists, and other allied social and applied science specialists are piecing together information drawn from investigations at local Hopewell residential sites that have long been overlooked to develop a better understanding of how these ancient people lived. They have been able to surmise what vegetables they grew, what they typically ate, how they created and dyed clothing, what they did for recreation, how they stored and cooked food, and how they built their homes.

Investigating an ancient home site near the Snake Den Complex.

Hey, That Sounds Like a Great Idea!

Those of you old enough to remember the television comedy *WKRP in Cincinnati* about a struggling radio station may remember an episode centered around an ill-fated Thanksgiving promotion where live turkeys were going to be dropped from a helicopter into a crowd of deserving people. There was only one problem with this promotion—turkeys can't fly.

The local Ashville Community Club and Nolan Amusements were looking to entice more people to celebrate their Fourth of July in Ashville, and they came across a great promotion that would be sure to bring more people to their carnival. The idea was simple—go to the local merchants and get coupons for free merchandise and have them kick in some cash to be loaded into a small rocket. The rocket would carry its payload several hundred feet, explode, and then send the contents raining down on the crowd below.

The days leading up to the Fourth of July were a marketing frenzy, with announcements of the money rocket everywhere in storefronts, the local press, and radio. The company that offered the promotion had performed it many times, so success was assured. Indeed, the day of the launch crowds packed into the park. Everyone was pushed back at least fifty feet from the launch pad. When the time came, everyone joined in on the countdown.

Ten, nine, eight, seven, six, five, four, three, two, one, liftoff! The crowd cheered as the craft hurtled high into the sky. But the rocket continued to go higher than expected, and when it finally exploded, a serious wind carried the money and the coupons into an adjacent housing area and even further into a farmer's corn field. People were climbing over fences, onto roofs, and into the corn field, destroying part of the crop. Good thing the promoters were insured.

Really great business ideas.

Okay, shooting off a rocket filled with prizes and money on a windy day is not a good idea. There are two people from the area, however, that did have really good ideas. So good, in fact, that the company one started is a top performer on the New York Stock Exchange and the other evolved into a top-ranked commercial brokerage firm on the Chicago Board of Trade. Both are Fortune 500 companies.

When Floyd Younkin saw the promise of fiber optics as a conduit for sending high-speed information, he decided that a company that could build the infrastructure for fiber optic networks would be in high demand. He was right. He started a company called Dycom. This is what *Fortune* magazine said about the company in 2016:

A major push for fiber-optic networks in homes and offices is behind the stellar growth at the Florida telecom service provider Dycom. The company is number 20 in Fortune magazine's list of America's 100 fastest growing companies.

Hal Richard established the Farmers Commodities Corporation as a major commodities company. FCStone acquired the fast-growing company in 2002 to serve midsized commercial clients. Today FCStone is a Fortune 500 financial services company providing trading and risk management for commodities, securities, foreign exchange, clearing and execution services, and global payments.

Optical Illusion?

From the 1870s through the early 1940s, there was a raging debate in the baseball world about whether a curveball really does curve or if it was just an optical illusion. Two major magazines sponsored tests in an effort to settle this debate. *Life* magazine determined from its tests that the curve was indeed an optical illusion. On the other side, *Look* magazine had time-lapse photographs indicating that "a curve ball actually does curve."

The Cleveland Indians had a superb curveball pitcher in Bob Feller. Feller was at the center of this debate. Was "Rapid Robert's" curveball so difficult to hit because it was an optical illusion? Well, in 1941 the *Cleveland Plain Dealer* was determined to get to the bottom of the controversy, so they called in Professor John G. Albright, a physicist from the Case School of Applied Science, to settle the dispute. Albright grew up near Ashville.

Dr. Albright bravely stood behind the Cleveland catcher while Feller threw thirty pitches. After it was over, Albright concluded that a curveball pitch actually does curve. Newspapers like the *Daily News* from New York and hundreds of others across America published Albright's pronouncement.

Bob Feller on a *Time* magazine cover

While Bob Feller made the cover of *Time* magazine, two local athletes, Russ Gregg and Don Thomas, made the April 5, 1948, *Life* magazine cover as Brooklyn Dodger rookies in training camp.

Both Russ and Don were stellar athletes in high school and signed as Dodgers. Russ played two years as a pitcher for the Dodgers, but a shoulder injury kept him from the big leagues. It was during spring training camp at Vero Beach, Florida, that he became friends with Jackie Robinson.

A 2007 story in the *Columbus Dispatch* recounts an incident with Jackie:

> *Jackie was playing eight-ball in the barracks with Billy Loes, who was our bonus-baby rookie at the time and a bit full of himself, and Billy called him a name—I think it was 'lammy pie,' which at that time was an expression for easy to beat—and Jackie got really upset,"* Gregg said.

> *Jackie got up in Billy's face and told him he didn't like being disrespected that way, and we had to separate them. After Billy left the pool hall, a lot of the guys cheered Jackie for standing up to Billy. That moment was completely out of character for Jackie. That was the only time I ever saw him get mad, and there were many, many times when he had reason to be.*

> *"Sure, you could sense the racism,"* he said. *"Some of the players in camp snubbed him, mostly notably the Southern kids, most of whom were just brought up under the mind-set that blacks and whites didn't belong together."*

Hearty Stock

John H. Sark was just following his normal duties as superintendent of the local canning factory when he lifted the gate of the elevator shaft. Only this time, when he lifted the gate and stepped onto the elevator, it was not there. He was paying attention to his paperwork when he stepped into the abyss, falling to the bottom of the multistory shaft to the horror of all who watched.

People rushed to his aid, but remarkably Sark appeared to have only minor injuries and returned to his duties. Despite his appearance, he soon fainted and was taken to his home to recuperate. Two days later he returned to work, but fell again, this time over pans placed on the floor to catch rainwater. He injured his hands.

Despite his injuries, he continued to perform his management responsibilities. As the local newspaper noted, "John does not halt for trifling athletic stunts that occur in the course of his duties."

In good running shape.

John Sark must have been in reasonably good shape. Falling down an elevator shaft would have killed or severely injured most individuals. One person from this area who tries to stay in good shape and uses humor to counsel others to do the same is Mark Remy.

Nathan Freeburg writes:

> *When it comes to running, writing about running, and laughing at those who run, Mark Remy has perfected the genre. You may know him from his four hilarious books about running, or as the author of the column "Remy's World" (online and in print from Runner's World), or perhaps from his most recent project, DumbRunner.com: an online destination for runners who enjoy laughter and pie.*

Mark has competed in twenty-six marathons and has written countless articles. He has contributed to *Runner's World* and was executive director of RunnersWorld.com. He has written for the *New Yorker*, *Men's Health*, and *Cosmopolitan*.

Mark running in the Boston Marathon

Bitter Rivals

The year was 1948. The game was between the highly touted Ashville Broncos and their number one rival in the Pickaway County Basketball League—the New Holland Bulldogs. The New Holland game was everything it was billed to be and was hotly contested. The game was so tight that it went into overtime. The score was New Holland over Ashville, 44–43, when the New Holland fans stormed the floor, sensing that the game was over.

New Holland's timekeeper contended that time had run out and the Bulldogs of New Holland had upset the undefeated Broncos. The Ashville timekeeper and the referees saw it differently.

Ashville immediately filed a protest with the State Commissioner of High School Athletics, Harold Emseiler, stating that referees had called a foul in the last seconds of the game against New Holland, but a crowd stormed the floor and the Ashville player was not allowed to complete his free throws. The commissioner ruled after hearing from all parties and obtaining a report from the referees of the game that New Holland's school administrators failed to allow the game to carry through to completion without crowd interference and with police protection if necessary. Ashville was awarded the victory 2–0, and New Holland was sharply reprimanded.

This was too much for the fans of New Holland. They were outraged by the commissioner's actions. An emergency session of the New Holland Boosters Club was called and they passed the following resolution:

> *Be it resolved, that a formal notice of protest be sent to all parties responsible for the atrocious reflections arbitrarily hurled upon our citizens, and that immediate*

steps be taken to explore the possibility of detaching the Village of New Holland from Pickaway County to annex the same to the County of Fayette, or to declare the Village of New Holland to be a separate and independent territory of the State of Ohio.

Had play ended before the foul was called? Until someone invents a time machine with instant replay, we will never know.

Time ran out—or did it?

In 1974 the Ohio State Buckeyes were undefeated and ranked No. 1 in the nation when they played at Michigan State. Ohio State was leading 13–9 with just five minutes left when Levi Jackson of MSU broke free for an eighty-eight-yard touchdown run. OSU drove down the field, confident that they could reach the goal line. With less than a minute left, they handed the ball to Teays Valley grad Champ Henson, the nation's leading scorer. Henson bulled his way near the goal line.

The officials did not indicate a touchdown, but there were twenty-nine seconds left. The Buckeyes attempted to line up again, but the Michigan State players laid on top of the pile up and prevented OSU from running another play. OSU argued that

Number 38 Champ Henson. Courtesy *Columbus Dispatch*

time out should have been called by the official—especially since Henson had made a first down, but none was called. The players reassembled for a final play, in which Brian Baschnagle reached the end zone. One official signaled that he scored, but another indicated that time had expired. The game was over. The Buckeyes' national championship hopes were dashed. Needless to say, Woody Hayes was not happy with the officials.

Chapter Seven

Close to the Stars

Although Ohio is not Beverly Hills, people do have occasional chance encounters with famous celebrities at Ohio's international airports. That is not what this chapter is about. It is about significant connections to celebrities.

The area celebrates a Scottish immigrant woman who lived in the Ashville area who was a dancing partner for the famed poet Robert Burns. A former Ashville resident entertained Al Capone and other Miami Beach gangsters, while hosting the movie stars of the 1920s in his hotel. A local lad found himself in *The Wizard of Oz* movie as a munchkin.

The biggest star in Ashville is the center star of a flag that was found in the attic of a home there. It turned out to be the oldest flag representing the State of Ohio.

Dean Bastian of Ashville directed many famous people and Hollywood celebrities like Alice Cooper during his tenure as creative director for national advertising agencies. Other recognizable names he has worked with include: Hal Holbrook, Mark Harmon, Sela Ward, Dick Cavett, Robin Leach, Jeff Probst, Lou Holtz, Nick Faldo, Mike Ditka, Joan Collins, Jon Gruden, Queen Latifah, David Spade, Tiger Woods, Phil Jackson, Steve Young, Jerry Rice, Chris Rock, and Barbara Eden.

Dancing with the Star

Andy Warhol supposedly said that "in the future, everyone will be world-famous for fifteen minutes." It led to the concept that almost all mass-media fame will be fleeting.

Margaret Shannon came to America as a young woman from Scotland in the late 1700s and ended up in Scioto Township. Her proudest moment came early in her life because her last dancing partner before she left for America was the famed Scottish poet Robert Burns.

Burns, his brother Gilbert, and some of their friends established a rural debating society in Tarbolton, Scotland, called the Bachelors' Club. The building where they held their debates was also the place where dancing and sewing classes were held. Burns joined a dancing club that met at the same building in 1779. That is supposedly where Margaret danced with Robert Burns.

Margaret lived to almost 104 years of age. She is the oldest person to have been buried in Commercial Point's Presbyterian cemetery and the only one buried there to have danced with the famous Robert Burns to the old folk song "O, when she cam ben she bobbed."

Teen dance-o-rama.

Margaret Shannon would not recognize the kind of dancing that Jerry Rasor hosted on WLWC (Channel 4). Jerry was a TV weatherman from Commercial Point. After a failed run for the US Congress in 1962, Jerry launched what musicologist George Gell called the second-longest and probably the second-most famous teen TV show in the state behind Cleveland's *Upbeat*. The show aired on Saturdays from eleven to twelve o'clock and featured the top ten records of the week, dance contests, and special guest recording artists, including local and national acts.

Jerry appears on a daytime soap opera.

Jerry's show was called *Dance Party* and *Teen Dance-O-Rama*, and it earned him local celebrity status. Not only did he get to rub elbows with famous people, but he also got to make his acting debut on NBC's daytime show *The Doctors*.

Jerry Rasor with Raquel Welch

Sons of the American Revolution guard the US transition flag.

Seventeen Stars–
Ohio's Oldest Flag

The state legislature of Ohio adopted a swallow-tailed flag designed by John Eisenmann as the state flag in 1902. It is the only non-rectangular state flag in the United States.

This flag was originally designed in 1901 to adorn the Ohio building at the Pan-American Exposition in Buffalo, New York. One of the members of the legislature, who was also a member of the Ohio Pan-American Exposition Commission, introduced a bill to designate Eisenmann's design as the only official flag representing the State of Ohio.

While it is true that Ohio did not have an official state flag until 1902, it was not the first flag to represent the state. After Ohio entered the Union of States in 1803, there were some US transitional flags designed that bore seventeen stars in honor of Ohio (Ohio was the seventeenth state to join the United States).

Perhaps the oldest and most iconic of these transitional flag designs in existence is located in Ohio's Small Town Museum in Ashville. The flag is handsewn with sixteen six-pointed stars in a circle and a star in the middle representing Ohio. The blue canton on which the stars were placed appears to be from an officer's uniform from the War of 1812.

The Siege of Detroit.

James Denny surveyed the town of South Bloomfield in 1803 for David Denny. He mustered troops from this area to fight in the War of 1812. He was an important figure during the defense and ultimate surrender of Fort Detroit. Denny handed over his prisoners of war and was released to Cleveland. He was later called to Congress to testify in the court martial of General William Hull and died in Philadelphia when traveling after appearing before Congress.

Here is a passage of correspondence to his wife foreshadowing what might happen to him and the Ohio militia in Detroit:

> *Dear Wife: I am yet safe, but am fearful this will not reach you to tell the news. When the Army retreated across the river to Canada, I was ordered to remain with about 250 men to finish a stockade work and maintain my post to the extremity ... We remained in place until the 11th and had made considerable improvements such as gave us every reason to hope that we could maintain our fort against any force, but we were ordered across the river and to evacuate the place immediately. ... Oh, if we had but a General [other than Hull]; we are lost; we are undone if nothing is done instantly. If this ever finds you it will be a miracle. Adieu,*
> *—Colonel James Denny*

Denny was awarded the rank of Brigadier General and lived in Circleville. He owned the first newspaper published in Pickaway County, *The Freedonia.*

The Accidental Munchkin

No one can say why James Reeves Hulse V's growth was stunted, but he had only reached a height of four feet six inches when he graduated from Muhlenberg Township High School in Darbyville. Jimmy loved school and was a Latin scholar. But the Depression and his size made it impractical for him to go to college. It looked like being a farm laborer was going to be his occupation.

Jimmy (left). Courtesy James Hulse Collection

But something occurred to interrupt his immediate plans. He happened to attend the Circleville Pumpkin Show and saw a program put on by the Harvey Williams Midget Troupe. Harvey noticed that Jimmy was also of a small stature. He made Jimmy an offer he could hardly refuse. The troupe was under contract to appear in a new movie called *The Wizard of Oz*, and they could guarantee him a role in the movie if he wanted to come along. Of course, Mr. Williams received a fee for everyone in his troupe who was in the film, so that meant more money for him.

Judy Garland and Toto

Many of the little people in *The Wizard of Oz* immigrated from Europe as part of Austrian Leo Singer's troupe and could not speak English well or take direction, so speaking and dancing parts were limited primarily to those who were American-born. Jimmy was thrilled to meet Judy Garland, but he was smitten by Carolyn Granger—a young lady in the Williams Troupe.

After the filming, Jimmy was offered additional work in another film that was to star some of the munchkins from *The Wizard*, but with no guarantees, he decided this was not the life for him and he returned home.

Jimmy continued as a farm laborer locally, but he later moved to Columbus with his mother and father. He worked at Frecker's Restaurant and a Tom Thumb restaurant. Later he worked at the George Byers & Sons Parking Garage. Still, he treasured his memory of working with Judy Garland on the set of *The Wizard of Oz*.

Other top 100 American films.

Jimmy is not the only one with local ties to have appeared in an iconic Hollywood film. Teays Valley High School

 teacher Charlie Kearns got his turn in the spotlight as the district attorney arresting the corrupt warden Samuel Norton and his toady Captain Byron Hadley in *The Shawshank Redemption*.

Sally Kellerman, who is the granddaughter of a former Ashville resident, was nominated for an Academy Award for her portrayal of nurse Margaret Houlihan in Robert Altman's movie *M*A*S*H*.

To Hell with Protocols

To say that President Jimmy Carter's brother, Billy, was his own man would be an understatement. Presidential protocol at inauguration ceremonies stipulates that immediate members of the family attending the event should be accompanied by a high-ranking military officer such as a general or admiral. This did not sit well with Billy. He wanted a friend who served with him in the Marines, Dan Barth, who grew up in Ashville, to do the honors. The following is a report from UPI (1977):

> *PLAINS, Ga (UPI)—Billy Carter, assigned a Marine officer as escort for inaugural ceremonies, said "to hell with that" and arranged for an old friend who was an enlisted man to do the honors. Carter and Marine Warrant Officer Dan Barth, of Columbus, Ohio, served together in the Marines for four years. Members of the president's family traditionally are escorted by high-ranking military officers.*

Dan and his wife, Cupia, joined Billy and Sybil Carter as they attended all the official inaugural events.

If only they had followed fire safety protocols.

Not all protocols are for appearance. There are some safety protocols that if not followed can kill people.

The Beverly Hills Supper Club was "the place to go" in the Midwest to see top-notch entertainers. It was a massive complex with fifty-four thousand square feet and nineteen rooms on two floors. By 1977, it was standard knowledge that you needed two years' advance notice to book an event at this legendary venue in Newport, Kentucky.

It was one place where you could just stroll into the bar and catch Redd Foxx, Rich Little, or other famous comedians perfecting their craft. There was no cover charge.

On the night of May 28, 1977, singer John Davidson was scheduled to perform before a sell-out crowd, when a fire broke out. The patrons in the over-capacity Cabaret Room (the main room) were not immediately informed of the fire. By the time they were, smoke and fire were beginning to engulf them. The building was a confusing maze to begin with, and it was constructed of wood and had no alarm or sprinkler system. There were not enough exits, according to the local fire code, and some exits were blocked. People had no way out.

That night there were 165 lives lost as the club burned to the ground. One of those lives belonged to John B. Beavers, a Teays Valley graduate, who was working as a supervisor at the Columbia Gas Distribution Company.

COMMONWEALTH OF KENTUCKY

BEVERLY HILLS SUPPER CLUB FIRE

Emergency squads came from miles around. Temporary morgue set up in nearby Ft. Thomas Armory. Families arrived for days searching for loved ones, as site smoldered. Story dominated the news. Probable cause was faulty aluminum wiring. Most people in area knew someone who lost family here. See reverse.

In memory of those who perished in the fire.

Al Capone and Ashville's Commodore Stoltz

While this area had its share of bootleggers and moonshiners, it did not rival the mobster activity found in places like Chicago or Miami Beach. That does not mean that this area had no connections to the racketeers who ruled those communities during Prohibition.

In the early 1920s, former Ashville resident Commodore Perry J. Stoltz helped Carl Fisher turn Miami Beach into a tourist mecca. Stoltz built and owned the fabulous Fleetwood Hotel, which had a beautiful roof garden that served as the entertainment spot in Miami. It was not uncommon to see the rich and famous taking in a live performance by crooner Eddie

Cantor. These shows would be broadcast nationally on Stoltz's radio station WMBF, which was also housed at the Fleetwood.

The shows at the Fleetwood also attracted gangsters like Al Capone who had winter homes on nearby Palm Island. Damon Runyon was assigned to cover the comings and goings of the mobsters and other celebrities who frequented these shows for various papers. Runyon was a well-respected sportswriter for Hearst News and a short-story writer who chronicled mob life. Some of these stories were the basis for the wildly successful musical *Guys and Dolls*.

While Stoltz steered clear of mob activity, he was a key witness to the murder of Duncan "Red" Shannon, who was known as the "Mad Mick," king of Florida rumrunners.

Apparently, the murder happened in front of Stoltz and two of his hotel guests, motion picture stars Bebe Daniels (*Maltese Falcon*) and Thomas Meighan (*Male and Female*).

On February 24, 1926, as the sun was setting over Miami Beach, Shannon approached the Hotel Floridian in his speedboat, called Goose. It was loaded with at least 170 cases of liquor. Shannon's boat was spotted by the crew of a Coast Guard patrol boat just south of Star Island. A chase ensued and witnesses say that Shannon and his crew had their hands up to surrender when the guardsmen fired on them, mortally wounding Shannon.

BBC commentator Alistair Cooke famously called Commodore Stoltz "that Miami Beach multi-millionaire with two-toned shoes."

A year before the murder, Stoltz was considered one of the wealthiest individuals in America, but that all came tumbling down when a hurricane hit Miami Beach. The storm killed hundreds of vacationers—ruining the flow of tourist dollars to the Fleetwood empire. Stoltz lost everything, including his marriage. Penniless, he moved back to Ashville to live with his mother.

Mural artist Dirk Rozich (on left) paid tribute to his two idols Walt Disney and Norman Rockwell by including them in the Ashville Fourth of July Mural—neither Walt or Norm has a local connection.

Chapter Eight

Mistaken

It is funny how many things are believed to be true just aren't. Don't eat and swim because it increases your risk of cramps—not true. Salty water boils quicker—not true. A flushed toilet rotates the other way in the Southern Hemisphere—not true.

The Ashville area has many stories that just are not true. In many cases what started out as speculation often became undisputed fact. Here are some examples:

Teddy Boor made the first traffic light—not true.

Vivian Michaels made the "Speedy" Alka-Seltzer puppet—not true.

John Holmes's real name was Jerry Wall and he lived on Long Street—not true.

The entertainer Roy Rogers worked at the local canning factory—not true.

James Hulse was the mayor of Munchkin Land—not true.

Walt Disney once lived here—not true, but he made it into a local mural anyway.

Mistaken Birthplace

One of the nineteenth century's most infamous murder cases involved Sarah Marie Victor. She supposedly poisoned her half-brother to collect on his insurance. In her book, *The Life Story of Sarah M. Victor for Sixty Years: Convicted of Murdering Her Brother, Sentenced to be Hung, Had Sentence Commuted, Passed Nineteen Years in Prison, Yet Is Innocent,* she related that she was born in Pickaway County. Several people familiar with her story believed she was born in Scioto Township.

Her father was a first-generation Frenchman who ran a store. He cosigned a note and that person defaulted, leaving him holding the bag. That failure drove him to near madness, and he left his wife and their very young children. His wife had to settle his debts after he abandoned them. After she appeased the debtholders, Sarah's mother moved them all to the Toledo area to seek better conditions. Sarah was about five years old when that happened.

The advent of Google, Ancestry.com, and other portals to access primary data proved that she was actually born in Piqua, Ohio. Her father, Joseph Parquet, purchased a tract of land near the Miami River in 1826. Sarah was born there on May 5, 1827. Interestingly, she mentions in her book that her birthplace was near the Miami River, but even her biographer never questioned that she might be wrong about Pickaway County.

So, Pickaway County and Scioto Township dodged a bullet.

There are other authors.

The Ohioana Library mistakenly identified Sarah Victor as one of only a few authors from Pickaway County. Actually, just this area of northern Pickaway County has a significant number of authors with publishing contracts and an even larger contingent of self-published authors.

The area's other prolific published authors include: botanist William Ashbrook Kellerman, environmental activist Gale Warner, theologian and poet Reverend Grover Swoyer, home economist and New York Times best selleing author Florence Brobeck, psychological thriller novelist Jennifer Rainey, novelist Tiffany McDaniel, Christian romance novelist Kathryn Alexander, fiction novelist Bethany DeVors, John Milton scholar Evertt M. Clark, theologian Reverend Mary Hinkle Shore, humorist and runner Mark Remy, geologist John Adams Bownocker, botanist William Ashbrook Kellerman, anti-domestic abuse advocate Larry Rinehart, science fiction and western novelist Wes Henson, anthologist Donna Jarrell, thriller novelist William D. Carl, psychological thriller novelist Jack Legg, and best selling novelist Michelle A. Valentine.

Mistaken Identity

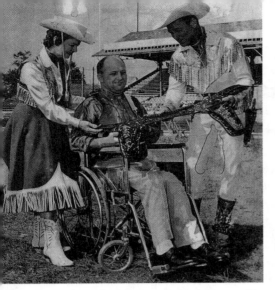

The real Roy Rogers and Dale Evans with leather crafter Boyd Kuhlwein

It has long been held that the famous singing cowboy Roy Rogers had a summertime job at the local canning factory in Ashville. Unfortunately, he was fired because he supposedly hid in a box car and played his guitar during work hours. Several residents swore they worked with the King of the Cowboys, and the local museum even developed a display about the incident.

After following up on several leads, a local researcher decided to call Mr. Rogers himself and get the full story. Roy and his daughter took his call in 1996. Roy stated he knew where Ashville was, but he never worked in that canning factory. He did work in a shoe factory in Cincinnati.

The researcher then checked to see what year the incident supposedly happened. It was between 1928 and 1930 when the young man who supposedly fired Roy Rogers managed the factory personnel. But the famous singing cowboy Roy Rogers had not changed his name from Leonard Slye yet. It was 1934, while singing with the Sons of the Pioneers, that he first used the name Dick Weston; he later chose the stage name Roy Rogers in honor of his childhood dentist.

So, who did the young man in charge of the cannery fire? Evidently, he fired a chicken thief named Roy Rogers, age

Holsters Boyd Kuhlwein made for Roy Rogers

forty-one, who lived in nearby South Bloomfield at the time. He spent time in the local Ashville jail for petty larceny and in the county jail for attempting to ship a crate of stolen chickens to Columbus.

The famous Roy Rogers did have a connection to Ashville. He had ornamental holsters that were made by a local leather crafter, Boyd Kuhlwein.

Where, oh where, are you tonight?

If you are a fan of the country-western comedy TV show *Hee Haw*, you will recognize this refrain. The song was written by Bob Newman, a member of the Georgia Crackers—RCA recording artists who shared billing with Roy Rogers and the Sons of the Pioneers. Ashville's Al Myers played lead guitar for the Crackers and recorded "Phfft! You Were Gone" with Bob for King Records on July 3, 1952.

Over the years, numerous country music writers and musicians have laid claim to this novelty classic, but the record shows that Bob Newman did indeed write the tune under his normal pseudonym (Lee Roberts) and King Records pressed the recording long before anyone else could buy the rights. Case closed!

The Crackers also appeared in four Columbia Pictures B movies featuring the Durango Kid during the last half of the 1940s.

Untrue Love Will Find a Way

National newspapers said that Kate Putnam and August Croft were ardent lovers who were born and reared on adjacent farms. Kate was fifteen years of age and August seventeen when he proposed, but family opposition and lack of money deferred the prospect of marriage. Still, they vowed to be true to each other.

They supposedly kept up a correspondence. Years rolled by, decades rolled by, but neither married another. The flame that had burned so passionately when they were younger did not flicker out.

After seventy-plus years, whatever barriers kept them apart were finally removed. The news spread quickly that the bachelor Croft and spinster Putnam were engaged to be married at the bride's home in South Bloomfield, Ohio. The wedding party was a large one, but no guest younger than sixty was invited. The minister was Reverend Moorehouse, who was a childhood friend of both parties.

The news of the long-lived sweethearts tying the knot made them celebrities of sorts. The notice of their wedding was celebrated in hundreds of newspapers across America.

While this story appeared nearly everywhere, including the *New York Times*, there is no evidence in the official records of Pickaway County that a Kate Putnam or August Croft lived here. There are no marriage, property, census, or cemetery records.

Find a way to love your community.

There is no evidence that the marriage of the aged lovebirds took place in South Bloomfield. However, there is plenty of evidence that people tied to this community, some of whom moved away, still love it. How else can you explain one of the poorer communities in Ohio annually providing a quarter of a million dollars in scholarships to graduating high school seniors? How can you explain building a state-of-the-art community library without any local, state, or federal tax dollars?

That is not all. It has already been noted that they have a nationally recognized museum that has never taken a dollar from the state or federal government. People have donated community park lands and land for senior housing.

The Floyd Younkin family gifted the community with a new library. The Richard and Mary Alice Peters family donated the Dreamland Theater for use as a museum. Guy and Louise Leatherwood donated land for the Louise Terrace senior citizen housing. Jerry Rasor saw to it that Commercial Point had a sizable park. Mary Jo Py and Judith Nicely provided funding for a community mural in honor of their parents Stanley and Ruth Bowers, and the Barr families set aside seventeen acres of land to preserve the Snake Den Mounds Complex.

The Barr family with videographer Gray Warriner (in the teeshirt)

Dejected Browns fan

Chapter Nine

Tall Orders

Sometimes people are called upon to find a solution to an intractable problem. Ohioans cannot figure out how to get the Cleveland Browns into the Super Bowl. Judging from past results, the Browns would do well to hire a team of people from the Ashville area skilled in finding solutions to difficult problems.

If there was a national award given for audacity in problem solving, there would be several strong candidates from this area. The Pickaway Bar Association's solution to potential sex discrimination was nothing if not brilliant. A local promoter's proposal to win the Indy 500 has to be one of the most intrepid approaches on record. Of course, one would have to acknowledge that locals charged with changing the direction of the Chicago River or starting a war with Spain also deserve consideration.

Solve This

When the Ashville law firm of Margulis Gussler Hall & Hosterman hired the first female lawyer in Pickaway County, it created a rather large problem for the all-male Pickaway County Bar Association. The former mayor of Ashville, Harry Margulis, had a bit of a reputation for supporting liberal causes, so it was not surprising that his firm hired Barbara Lucks, a talented young graduate from law school.

Barb had only been with the firm a short time when Harry invited her to come to the Pickaway County Bar Association luncheon. By virtue of having passed the bar, she was a member, but she was not welcomed by all.

After a brief business meeting, one member was trying to gauge how many were interested in attending the Bar Association's outing to a Cincinnati Reds baseball game. When Barbara raised her hand, the room fell silent.

The thought that a woman might actually attend an association outing was an affront to nearly all the older barristers present. For historic reasons, the bar had passed a resolution that no women were allowed on these outings. Now it was clear that there was a problem.

After the silence and then the rising undercurrent of talking by those still in favor of the "no women" rule, Harry stood up, waited for the room to quiet again, and said two words: "She goes." The members were faced with an impasse, but fortunately someone proposed a resolution that solved the barristers' problem:

"For the purposes of the Pickaway County Bar Association, Barbara J. Lucks is not a woman."

Motion passed. Problem solved.

Ashville's Atticus Finch and New Jerusalem.

Ashville has had more than its share of amazing events, but the election of Harry Margulis as mayor in 1936 has to be near the top. Harry was a young Jewish lawyer, the son of Russian immigrant parents, who had set up practice in town only five years after the local Ku Klux Klan klavern conducted parades and burned crosses around the town—especially in front of the school or the homes of people they hoped to scare away. They warned about the perilous impact of blacks, Catholics, and Jews on their way of life—diluting their culture.

In the 1880s there were ninety African Americans living in the area. By 1920 there was only one. There were only a handful of Jewish and Catholic families who dared to live in the area in the 1930s, and it was more than apparent that locals were not in the mood to welcome any more into the community.

Despite being Jewish in a community dominated by white Protestant sentiments, Harry decided to run for mayor in 1935—just two years after moving to Ashville. Harry grew up in Columbus selling items in his father's men's store. It helped him develop a charismatic charm that later earned the respect and admiration of local residents. He took on difficult cases and developed a reputation as an effective attorney. But no one gave him a chance to pull off a victory. Harry did not back down, and against all odds, he won by twenty-five votes over the incumbent. His victory was not without some controversy, as some pranksters covered the name "Ashville" on the corporate limit sign and replaced it with "New Jerusalem."

Make the Chicago River Flow Backward

In 1885 the residents of Chicago experienced the deaths of ninety thousand persons from cholera—almost 10 percent of the city's population—because their raw sewage was dumping into the Chicago River and then into Lake Michigan, which was the source of their drinking water. But what could possibly be done to solve this problem? Well, a Chicago commission came to the conclusion that the best solution was to reverse the flow of the Chicago River and send the sewage through the Illinois River down to the Mississippi.

Isham Randolph changed the direction of the Chicago River.

This difficult engineering feat incorporated a system of rivers and canals with a combined length of more than 150 miles. In 1999 this system was named a "Civil Engineering Monument of the Millennium" by the American Society of Civil Engineers.

The person charged with overseeing the construction of a series of canals and locks to accomplish this feat was the City of Chicago's Chief Civil Engineer, Isham Randolph. Twenty years earlier, Mr. Randolph had been largely responsible for the engineering and construction of the Scioto Valley Railroad through Walnut and Harrison Townships. He lived with the William Cromley family in Ashville during the surveying and construction of the line.

Isham Randolph's engineering achievements earned him a great deal of respect. He was appointed to the International Board of Consulting Engineers for the construction of the Panama Canal in May of 1905 by President Theodore Roosevelt.

Randolph, Joseph Ripley, and Alfred Nobel were largely responsible for issuing a minority report differing from the Board of Consulting Engineers' majority support that argued for a sea-level plan. Instead, they proposed a lock-

Board of Consulting Engineers with Isham Randolph. Courtesy Isham Randolph Collection

and-dam system. Randolph was publicly denounced in the national press for being disloyal, but his team's argument ultimately caused Roosevelt to change his mind. As historian David Rogers noted:

In this unexpected shift (by Roosevelt) the Americans would avoid the colossal catastrophe that might have occurred, that they attempted a sea level canal across the Continental Divide at Culebra, where some of the world's largest landslides had yet to occur.

The man who engineered the construction of the Scioto Valley Railroad through Ashville and boarded with the Cromleys, the man who changed the direction of the Chicago River and convinced President Teddy Roosevelt to adopt a design for the Panama Canal that used a series of locks and dams has a street in Ashville with his name on it—Randolph Street.

Bring About Racial Equality

Well now, there is a tall order. At the end of WWII, black American leaders were pushing the Truman administration to desegregate the US armed forces. White Americans were generally not ready to accept that black Americans deserved to be treated equally.

After WWII, the Tuskegee Airmen were stationed at Lockbourne Army Air Base, not far from Ashville. It was one place in America where African American officers commanded white civilian employees, and it was done without serious conflicts erupting. They earned the respect of their support staff.

This was no easy task, as nearby Ashville had only years before elected to become a sundown town, where blacks were not allowed after dark. The success of the Tuskegee Airmen officers in directing the predominately white civilian support employees allowed President Truman to finally issue the order to desegregate the armed services. Lockbourne, under base commander Colonel Benjamin O. Davis Jr., became the model for racial integration of the armed forces.

Benjamin Davis Jr. became the first black US Air Force general, the 322nd Fighting Wing of the Tuskegee Airmen became celebrated war heroes and champions for racial equality, and the desegregation of the armed services at Lockbourne became a significant milestone in the struggle for racial justice.

Pearl Farrow's war.

Pvt. Pearl T. Farrow was the son of William T. Farrow and Sarah Williams and grew up in Scioto Township, sometimes working as a farm laborer. Pearl was considered to be of mixed race, according to his enlistment papers, so he became a member of Company L in the 813th Pioneer Infantry Regiment—an African American unit.

The all-African American 813th Pioneer Infantry regiment was organized and trained at Camp Sherman and would wind up with the US Second Army in France in 1918. Farrow died overseas on November 15, 1918—just four days after Armistice ended the war—of tubercular bronchopneumonia. His body was returned to the United States and was buried in Greenlawn Cemetery, Chillicothe, Ohio.

Influenza at home and overseas killed many WWI soldiers.

Any dreams that Pearl and his fellow African American comrades had that their involvement in the war would result in fair and equal treatment for their race were dashed. Blacks returned home from the war, and racial violence increased.

African American troops at Camp Sherman. Courtesy Ohio History Connection

Make Spain Declare War on the United States

After the explosion and sinking of the USS *Maine* on February 15, 1898, in Havana, Cuba, and the "yellow" journalism that followed blaming the incident on Spain, the United States began blockading the port at Havana. President McKinley hoped that Spain would be driven to declare war on the United States and that the US Congress would follow suit. McKinley also had the US Navy engage in the capture of Spanish vessels.

Buoy from the battleship *Maine*

There had been several small vessels taken by the Navy, but none of these prizes seemed to enrage the Spanish enough to finally declare war. However, Ensign H. H. Christy commanded a boarding crew from the USS *New York* and the USS *Detroit* that captured the Spanish ocean liner *Catalina*. This act was so blatant that the Spanish embassy cabled Madrid, and within hours Spain declared war on the United States. The United States reciprocated the next day by declaring war on Spain.

In the end, the United States paid Spain $20 million for Guam, Puerto Rico, Spanish possessions in the West Indies, and the Philippines. The United States occupied Cuba but did not annex it. Victory in the Spanish American War transformed the United States into an imperial power.

We need to declare peace.

H. H. Christy was present at the beginning of the Spanish American War. In a weird twist of fate, he was also involved in the end of another war.

After the sinking of the *San Diego* during WWI, then-Captain H. H. Christy was given command of the USS *Wyoming*. He was one of six naval commanders chosen to escort President Woodrow Wilson after he crossed the Atlantic to the harbor at Brest, France, to sign the Treaty of Versailles, ending WWI.

Did we need to imprison the guiltless?

On March 18, 1942, FDR issued Executive Order 9102, which led to the forced relocation of approximately 110,000 Japanese-Americans living on the West Coast. More than two-thirds of these people were native-born American citizens. They were confined in inland internment camps operated by the civilian War Relocation Authority. Only one Japanese-American male was given an honorable exemption—the former personal steward of Admiral H. H. Christy, Inomata Kingi. This was even more remarkable because Inomata was a naturalized citizen who was born in Japan.

Inomata Kingi, steward to Admiral H. H. Christy. Courtesy Kinji Inomata III

Johnny Lightning race team. Jim Cook is standing fourth from the left in a sweater. Courtesy Jim Cook Collection

Find an Indy 500 Sponsor

South Bloomfield resident Jim Cook was a Firestone representative trying to line up a major sponsorship for the Parnelli Jones racing team's run at the 1970 Indianapolis 500. He was trying to convince the toy company Mattel to provide a Hot Wheels sponsorship, but they declined. At that time Mattel had a lot of Hot Wheels promotions going, and the Indy 500 was not televised. Besides, the idea seemed a little crazy to them.

That rejection did not deter Jim. He marched his idea over to Topper Toys' founder Henry Orenstein. Topper had a metal car called "Johnny Lightning," but its sales were sluggish in comparison to Hot Wheels.

Sports Illustrated recounted a memorable meeting in 1969, eleven months before Indy, between Orenstein and Cook. Orenstein asked Jim, "If your head was on the chopping block and your life depended on giving me the right answer, tell me now, who is going to win the Indy 500 next year?" Cook responded immediately, "Al Unser." That was all Orenstein needed to hear. He signed on to sponsor five racing cars that were to be called "Johnny Lightning Specials." They were to be painted blue with gold lightning bolts.

Jim thought he had hit a home run, but some on the team thought that having a toy company sponsor an Indy car would make them a laughing stock in the racing community. But he got the last laugh when Al Unser won the 1970 Indy 500. Seeing the Johnny Lightning toy car sales take off in direct competition with Hot Wheels also put a smile on his face. Then the Johnny Lightning team did the unthinkable. They won it again in 1971.

What's after winning?

After winning the Indy 500, Jim Cook went on to manage the Ontario Motor Speedway in Ontario, California, and later was a PGA tournament official. His love of golf transferred to both his son, John, and his daughter, Cathy. John won eleven times on the PGA tour and was a member of the 1993 Ryder Cup team. Today he is a studio analyst on the Golf Channel. Cathy was a stellar player on The Ohio State University women's golf team.

In 1992 the Cook family pooled their collective resources to acquire and develop farmland bordering the Scioto River and Walnut Creek. John worked with famous golf course architects Dr. Michael Hurdzan and Dana Fry to shape the stimulating course.

It is known as one of the best public courses in central Ohio. It has been a top pick for public golf courses by the Columbus Dispatch for several years.

The golf course is bordered by 140 acres of wetlands and wildlife habitat. The preservation of these features resulted in the course receiving several national environmental design awards.

Bring More Excitement to Indy Racing

You could say that Sarah Fisher was born to race cars. It all started when, at the age of four, she was given a Barbie pedal car. When she turned eight years old, she joined the World Karting Association. She won its Grand National Championship when she was eleven, twelve, and fourteen years old. It wasn't long until she was racing midget cars. Not only was she winning races against talented older male drivers, she also set a track record at Winchester Speedway. This all happened while she was graduating from Teays Valley High School as a top student and a member of the National Honor Society.

Her victory at Winchester attracted the attention of the Indy Racing League. Soon after transitioning from dirt track racing to asphalt, she qualified for the Indianapolis 500. She became the third and youngest woman to do so. Qualifying for the Indy 500 at such a young age garnered her at lot of attention from national media. She became the darling of the open-wheel racing world—even earning Driver of the Year accolades, which brought more fans.

Although she was not able to win an IndyCar race as a driver, she was the first woman to earn a pole position and the first to earn a place on the podium with a second-place finish. When she retired as a driver in 2010, she turned her focus to being an IndyCar team owner. She was the first woman team owner whose team won an IndyCar race.

In May of 2011 Sarah was appointed to a three-year term on the National Women's Business Council, an advisory council to both the president of the United States and Congress. She also cowrote *99 Things Women Wish They Knew before Getting Behind the Wheel of Their Dream Job.*

Karting classic.

Sarah Fisher is from Commercial Point, and since she was a three-time world champion go-karter before she even turned fifteen, it seems fitting that Commercial Point would reembrace its long-standing tradition of hosting the Commercial Point Karting Classic. Go-kart racing in the streets of Commercial Point started in 1968, but it continued sporadically over the years. The current Karting Classic entered its ninth year in 2019. Proceeds from the Classic benefit youth programs in Pickaway County.

The Classic has one of the richest purses in the country, with $10,000 in guaranteed payouts. But guess what? Admission for viewing the Classic is free. Races are held rain or shine.

Commercial Point Homecoming.

The Commercial Point Homecoming has been going strong since 1937. Every year the Commercial Point Community Men's Club puts on a three-day event that includes free entertainment, midway rides, Friday night fireworks, a car show, a beer garden, and a wide variety of food, but locals will tell you that you will miss out if you fail to try one of their fried fish sandwiches. Locals will tell you the same thing at the Ashville Fourth of July.

Reminder of the sacrifices made during WWII at the Luxembourg American Cemetery.

Chapter Ten

Coming to the Aid of Others

Americans have a long history of aiding others in the grip of war or other calamities. People from the Ashville area have willingly risked their lives to help others. Many of these brave people connect the community to major events in the history of our country.

This chapter highlights some of their actions and honors their sacrifice. In this regard, Ashville is no different from any other community in America.

The Battle of Adobe Walls

Dr. George S. Courtright of Walnut Township served in the army as a post surgeon at Fort Sumner on the Pecos River. The *California Column* recounts another role of the surgeon and physician:

> *He was also surgeon for the campaign in the expedition commanded by Brigadier General Christopher "Kit" Carson against the Comanches and Kiowa Indians and was engaged at the battle of the Adobe Walls, November 25, 1864.*

The First Battle of Adobe Walls ended in a victory for the Comanche–Kiowa alliance and was the last military engagement for General Carson, who retreated with his troops to New Mexico. If he had not retreated, a massacre worse than Custer's Last Stand might have resulted. It all

began when Carson attacked and destroyed a Kiowa village of 176 lodges. As he moved his troops toward Adobe Walls, a large group of Comanche and Kiowa warriors began to assemble against them. A fierce battle ensued. Carson's small contingent was running low on ammunition, so he ordered a retreat. Those involved with Carson called it a "brilliant affair." It was brilliant, in a way, because Carson escaped with his life, and today he has a state capital named in his honor—Carson City, Nevada.

Wounded Knee massacre.

Archaeologist Warren King Moorehead was responsible for the 1897 study of the Snake Den Mounds. He returned to Snake Den from New Mexico, where he was recuperating from tuberculosis in the fall of 1897, to verify the findings of his understudy, Dr. Clarence Loveberry.

This was just seven years after the traumatic events at Wounded Knee. Moorehead had fought hard to preserve historic Native American cultures in the United States, but his personal efforts to avert tragedy at the Pine Ridge Indian Reservation, where he was working closely with the Lakota people, failed. He was forcefully removed on December 28, 1890, by the US Cavalry. The next day, nearly all of the native people he had come to know and admire were massacred by the US government. It was a devastating event that haunted him for the rest of his life.

Fleeing Slavery

People often ask whether the Underground Railroad had any connection to the Ashville area. The answer is a resounding YES. The area had conductors and station masters primarily associated with the antislavery United Brethren Church. They helped fugitive slaves traveling north up the Scioto Valley.

The church took a strong stand against slavery in 1821. After 1837, slaveowners were no longer allowed to remain as members of the United Brethren Church. In 1847 the United Brethren founded Otterbein University after meeting at the UB Bethlehem Church in Walnut Township. Members of the UB church in Pickaway County were known conductors on the Underground Railroad.

Reverend William Hanby was on the search committee that was established at that meeting to find appropriate property to develop a college. They ended up selecting a site in Westerville, Ohio, for Otterbein. Hanby was located in Circleville and also traveled to the many congregations in the Ashville area to preach. His son Benjamin wrote the famous antislavery song "Darling Nelly Gray."

Dichotomy.

The question is how could a community that supported the Underground Railroad, flocked to see *Uncle Tom's Cabin* at Steward's Opera House, and employed many freed slaves as farm laborers and domestic help turn around a generation later and adopt sundown ordinances to scare African Americans away, cheer D. W. Griffith's silent film *Birth of a Nation*, and embrace the Ku Klux Klan? How could they shun Catholics and Jews, but elect the only Jewish man in town as their mayor? How could many of them go to work under and accept the administration of African American Air Force officers? The answer is not a simple one because local opinions about racial equality and religion are not homogenous.

The community acceptance and support for a thirteen-year-old African American child in foster care with an Ashville family turned into something more when that child grew into a positive youth leader and promising athletic prospect. Walter Stewart graduated from Teays Valley as the captain of his team and accepted an athletic

Walter Stewart with his foster family

scholarship to the University of Cincinnati, where he was an outstanding leader and team player. While he was unable to pursue a career as a professional football player because of a congenital condition, he focused on becoming a defensive line coach.

The Cincinnati grad started his coaching career as a graduate assistant defensive line coach at Tennessee. He moved on to become the defensive line coach at Eastern Kentucky and Northern Illinois, and he now works in that position at Temple University.

Viva la Revolución?

After the Civil War, Major John Thomas of Ashville was appointed Superintendent of the National Cemetery at Lebanon, Kentucky, and later of the San Antonio National Cemetery in Texas. In 1905 he was named the Superintendent of the US National Cemetery in Mexico City. There were 1,529 persons interred at this two-acre site—the only property in Mexico City owned by the US government. Thomas was directed to erect an iron fence around the site and build a tool house, a water system, and a new house for the superintendent's family.

By 1911 he was writing friends back home with news of the revolutionaries in different parts of Mexico. He was concerned that reports of the fighting were being muzzled by the Mexican government. Any newspaper that failed to comply with the gag order was summarily placed out of business. John noted:

We depend on railroad men for information. These men seem to be reliable; they give us the news every day, and if half of it is true, this government will pass into a fog before many moons. The rebels are getting the best of the troops in nearly all the engagements. Such conditions make us put on our thinking caps and to blow through our Winchesters to see that there are no cobwebs in them.

The manifest destiny war.

Major Thomas noted that all of the men interred at the US National Cemetery died on Mexican soil during the Mexican-American War (1846–1848). As was mentioned earlier, the first US flag representing Ohio, which is now in the possession of Ohio's Small Town Museum, is connected to both that war and the War of 1812.

There is another aspect to this that is not generally known. An Ashville-area man living in Madison Township was an Ohio representative in the US Congress when newly elected US President James K. Polk, a Democrat, moved to annex Texas as the first step towards a further expansion of the United States—our manifest destiny. Mexico was not happy with this act and attacked US forces sent to the disputed area. Polk and his allies in Congress viewed this as a convenient act of war. They also saw it as an opportunity to annex additional Mexican territory (what is now New Mexico, Arizona, Nevada, and California).

Democrat representative Augustus Perrill, from Ohio's Ninth District, cast his vote to declare war against Mexico. Nearly all of the Ohio Democrats voted to declare war, but the Whig representatives were less inclined to do so. Nevertheless, Congress passed a bill authorizing the president to employ military forces against Mexico on May 13, 1846.

US Representative
Augustus Perrill

9-11 Attack on the Pentagon

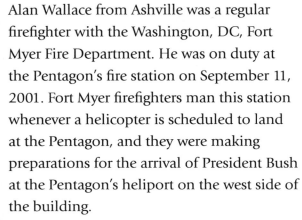

Alan Wallace from Ashville was a regular firefighter with the Washington, DC, Fort Myer Fire Department. He was on duty at the Pentagon's fire station on September 11, 2001. Fort Myer firefighters man this station whenever a helicopter is scheduled to land at the Pentagon, and they were making preparations for the arrival of President Bush at the Pentagon's heliport on the west side of the building.

Here is part of his firsthand account of the plane striking the Pentagon:

Mark and I continued to mess around the fire truck. The last minute or two before the plane hit the Pentagon, Mark and I were working in the right rear compartment where the foam metering valves are located. . . . We had walked past the right front corner of the crash truck (Foam 161) and were maybe 10–15 feet in front of the truck when I looked up toward my left side. I saw a large frame commercial airliner crossing Washington Blvd., heading towards the west side of the Pentagon! The plane had two big engines, appeared to be in level flight, and was approximately 25 feet off the ground, and about 200 YARDS from our location.

A lot of smoke was in the sky above the Pentagon. The rear of the crash truck was on fire with a large blaze. But most noticeable was that everything around the fire truck on the ground was on fire. Also, the west side of the Pentagon was on fire, from the first to the fifth (top) floor.

Planting corn at the Pentagon.

There was a time when the land upon which the Pentagon now sits was farmland used by the US Department of Agriculture. The Arlington Farm property was used by the Bureau of Plant Industry, headed up by Dr. Fredrick D. Richey, to test varieties of corn and methods of production. He is credited with developing inbreds 6-5, CI4-8, and L9 at the Arlington Farm. Here is a University of Tennessee Department of Plant Sciences tribute to Dr. Richey:

Dr. F. D. Richey, whose forty-three years spent in corn breeding research earned him national recognition for putting the hybrid corn industry where it is today. A graduate of the University of Missouri, Dr. Richey joined the USDA in 1911 and in 1922 was appointed Agronomist in Charge of Corn Investigations in the Bureau of the Plant Industry. He became chief of the bureau in 1934. The USDA Distinguished Service Award was given to Dr. Richey in 1948.

Dr. Richey lived on Main Street in Ashville while he worked with Roger Hedges in the development of Hedges Hybrids Seed Corn. Richey was an avid proponent of inbred lines of corn using a technique he had developed called "convergent improvement." Roger Hedges was a visionary agronomist who saw the promise of improved breeding for commercial seed corn.

Saving Captain Phillips

There are few events that totally grip the nation like the plight of
Apollo 13, Baby Jessica, or the 9-11 attack. Beginning April 8th, 2009,
Americans found themselves totally spellbound by events taking
place about four hundred miles off the coast of Somalia. Four armed
Somali pirates boarded the maritime ship *Maersk Alabama* and
attempted to seize the vessel. Their attempts were thwarted by the
crew but the pirates seized Captain Richard Phillips and launched a
lifeboat with him onboard. The pirates hoped to reach their mother
ship but lost contact with it.

It did not take long until they were intercepted by the US Naval
destroyer USS *Bainbridge*. Captain Frank Castellano and his officers,
including Logan Karshner from Ashville, were instructed to prevent
the pirates from reaching the Somali coast. They negotiated for
Captain Phillips's release at the same time Navy SEALs were
parachuted in to intervene if necessary. Castellano and the SEAL Team
continued to try to find a peaceful solution as they took the drifting
lifeboat under tow. The lead pirate agreed to board the *Bainbridge*
to negotiate for Phillips's ransom, but this was a ruse, and the pirate
commander was captured.

Phillips's ordeal came to an end on day five, when the Navy SEALs
were forced to shoot and kill the three pirate kidnappers remaining
on the lifeboat. They had just threaten to kill Captain Phillips.

It was a harrowing time for all of the crew and officers aboard
the *Bainbridge*, but in the end Captain Phillips was recovered alive.
For Karshner the scariest moments came earlier in the drama when
Phillips attempted to escape the lifeboat. It was a moonlit night when
he jumped overboard, but the pirates started shooting at him and he
was pulled back into the lifeboat. Karshner was afraid the pirates had
shot and killed their prisoner.

Can I have lobster?

The Blaney family was taking a leisurely canoe trip down the Olentangy River when they came upon a small dam. The canoe carrying nine-year-old Diana overturned and she was caught in the dam's hydraulic churn. The turbulent water swept her under and prevented her father from reaching her.

When the Sharon Township firefighters arrived on the scene, they were able to locate her bobbing head and lifeless body. They immediately used their water rescue equipment to pull her limp body from the river, while the cries of her father pierced the constant roar of the churning water: Save my child. Save my child. It is a panic-stricken, helpless moment no parent ever wants to experience.

Firefighter Gary Wing lifted her body up to the bank and began to clear her airways and breathe into her. Others thought he was too late to save her, but he kept on and was not going to stop until the medics could arrive and take over. The medics were able to reestablish her breathing, but she was hospitalized and placed on a respirator for several days.

Years later, Gary was curious about what happened to the little rag doll of a girl that nearly drowned that day. It turned out that she not only recovered without any brain damage but was now a revered scientist working at NASA on various space exploration projects. They were able to reconnect at a Columbus-area restaurant more than forty years after the incident.

Gary asked her what she remembered about the events surrounding her near-death experience. She could not recall much, but she did remember that when she finally woke up, the doctor told her she could eat anything she wanted. She asked for lobster.

D-Day Invasion

There are several young men from the area whose lives were lost in the effort to win the fight against the Axis powers during WWII. Each one exhibited acts of uncommon courage in performing their duties in the field of battle and the theater of war. Each deserves more than the faint praises exhibited here:

Pvt. William J. Schlarp at Omaha Beach. Pvt. Schlarp, of 5040 East Main Street in South Bloomfield, died of wounds received during the D-Day invasion at Omaha Beach. He was in A Company of the 16th Infantry Regiment. The 16th was in the first wave to storm the beach and took a high number of casualties.

Family photos of Pvt. William Schlarp. Courtesy Melissa Mabe

Battle of the Bulge

Pvt. Grant E. Puckett. Pvt. Puckett served in the 309th Infantry Regiment, 78th Infantry Division during WWII. His father was a farm laborer whose family lived various places in Pickaway County, but they were living on a Duvall Road farm in Harrison Township when Grant enlisted. He perished on January 11, 1945, during the Battle of the Bulge.

The 309th and 310th Infantry Regiments took over for parts of the 1st Division on the frontline near Entenpfuhl in early December. On the 13th, these regiments tore through Simmerath, Witzerath, and Bickerath and were fighting for Kesternich when Field Marshal von Rundstedt launched his counteroffensive on the 18th of December. The 78th held

the territory it had taken from the Siegfried Line against the ferocious German attacks that winter.

Grant's remains are interred at the World War II Netherlands American Cemetery, in the village of Margraten in the southernmost part of the Netherlands. It is administered by the American Battle Monuments Commission. Grant's monument is located in Plot C Row 6 Grave 29.

Pvt. William Frederick Hinton. Pvt. Hinton was born September 14, 1923, near Robtown to Cyrus and Bessie Furniss Hinton. He served in the infantry. He was killed in action on the first day of the German offensive we call the Battle of the Bulge, which lasted from December 16, 1944, to January 25, 1945. This was the last major German campaign on the Western Front during WWII.

Luxembourg Battle of the Bulge Memorial

The surprise attack caught the Allied forces completely off guard. American forces bore the brunt of the attack and incurred their highest casualties of any operation during the war. The battle also severely depleted Germany's armored forces, and they were largely unable to replace them. German personnel and, later, Luftwaffe aircraft (in the concluding stages of the engagement) also sustained heavy losses.

Hürtgen Forest Battle

Pvt. Jarold Raymond Roese. Pvt. Roese was born March 12, 1922, to Ira and Nellie (Shonkwiler) Roese in South Bloomfield. He grew up in Millport and died near Aachen, Germany, during the Battle of Hürtgen Forest on November 17, 1944. This battle is considered one of the grittiest combat actions of World War II. The battle still holds the record as the longest land engagement in US Army history.

Jarold was part of the allied assault into the Hürtgen Forest that was intended to allow the Army to capture the Ruhr Valley's industrial centers. The initial American thrusts in late September and early October centered on the village of Schmidt. The terrain in the area was treacherous and difficult to penetrate. The casualties during the first three weeks of fighting were exceedingly high, with more than 4,500 American troops killed and wounded.

Battle for Cassino

Sgt. Earl A. White. Sgt. White, of Ashville, was with the 36th Infantry Division. He was presumed killed at Cassino, Italy, fighting entrenched German positions in one of the worst tactical losses of the war. Earl had just finished his sophomore year at Ashville when he enlisted. Here is a firsthand account of what happened at Cassino:

Everybody in the 36th was getting hammered. Around 4 a.m., the Germans hurled 300 shells at the division's command post, causing casualties and disrupting the division's staff work. Rumors spread that the Germans were counterattacking and making their own river crossing (Rapido River) to trap the Americans. They were not, but heavy river currents washed away two footbridges weakened by German shells. The men of the 36th were tired, wounded, lost, and hungry. By 4 p.m., every commander in both battalions on the far shore was dead or wounded, and a German shell hit the last footbridge, obliterating it.

Between 6 p.m. and 7 p.m., 40 men paddled their way to the near bank, clinging to logs and debris to propel themselves through the bitterly cold current. Everyone else on the other side was left to be killed or captured. After about 8 p.m., the sounds of gunfire died down on the far side. The 1st/141st was annihilated. The 36th Division suffered more than 430 killed, 600 wounded, and 875 missing. Most of the missing were presumed killed or captured.

Battle of Iwo Jima

Sgt. Elmer A. Neff. Sgt. Neff was born to Clark and Mable (Toole) Neff on February 17, 1924, at Millport, Ohio. He attended Ashville-Harrison schools and was active in sports. Tall and muscular, he was a natural basketball player. He played center on both the reserve and varsity teams.

Elmer was a member of Company C, 1st Battalion, 24th Marine Regiment, 4th Marine Division. He and his fellow corpsmen landed on Iwo Jima on February 19, 1945, in what became known as the "Curtain of Hell." The 4th Division landing zone stretched north from halfway up the shoreline to the high cliffs above the East Boat Landing. From the high ground looking down on this beach, the Japanese troops under the command of General Kuribayashi sprang a counterattack that made the 4th Division easy targets for a downpouring of mortars, artillery, and machine gun fire. It was a killing ground, but Elmer managed to survive.

On the tenth day of the fight, six of his company, including his best friend, Glenn Buzzard, were under fire in a shell hole. An incoming mortar killed all of them except his shell-

Charlie Company survivors after Iwo Jima

shocked buddy. Buzzard handed Elmer his .38 pistol and told him to keep it until he got back. Buzzard blacked out but was carried to a location where he could recover.

On March 7—the seventeenth day of the battle—Sgt. Neff and his men mounted an attack on the desolate Turkey Knob. The fighting was fierce, and Neff was mortally wounded. One of his comrades retrieved the .38 pistol and gave it back to Buzzard days later when he returned to the front, together with the sad news that his friend did not survive.

Air Losses

1st Lt. Charles W. Mayberry at Grosseto, Italy. Lt. Mayberry was a P-47 fighter pilot in the 66th Fighter Squadron, 57th Fighter Group stationed in Italy. He was a 1939 graduate of Walnut High School. He had already completed numerous missions in the Italian theater when he took his plane, *Little Kitten*, on a run to test his engine. The plane took off from the Grosseto Main airfield, but the engine timing failed shortly after becoming airborne. The plane plummeted to the ground, killing the young lieutenant.

2nd Lt. Richard A. Hedges at Pocatello, Idaho. Hedges graduated from The Ohio State University, having authored agricultural research articles. He became the pilot of a B-24 in the 776th Bomber Squadron, 464th Bomber Group. His aircraft was making a practice bombing run out of the Pocatello Army Airfield on a target from twenty thousand feet when the crew experienced engine trouble and went into a spin.

After a harrowing three-minute descent, Hedges was able to pull the craft out of the spin five hundred feet off the ground. Unfortunately, the stress of the spin weakened the superstructure, and the left rudder tore off, sending the aircraft out of control and killing all seven on board.

Recent recovery work has taken place at the Idaho National Laboratory to identify material from the wreckage.

Jellico Train Disaster

Pvt. John R. Wickline and Pvt. Robert Prindle of Orient in the Jellico Train Disaster. Both privates had just finished basic training and were headed to their first assignment to an army unit at Fort Benning, Georgia. The late-night Louisville and Nashville Railroad train that carried them and 1,004 other new recruits jumped the tracks and plunged into the Clear Fork River. The train was ripped in half. The engine, tender, and four cars smashed into the rocks of the Jellico Narrows in Campbell County, Tennessee. John was killed in the accident and Bob was knocked unconscious with serious wounds.

High-Priority Vietnam MIA/POW

Eugene Lacey Wheeler grew up in Ashville. He was co-valedictorian of his high school class and played shortstop on the high school baseball team. He did not have an easy life growing up. Both of his parents died before he was seven years old. His grandmother raised him with six other brothers and sisters in a small house on Jefferson Avenue. He and his brother James delivered the *Columbus Dispatch*.

Lacey joined the service soon after graduation. He was quickly identified as a potential pilot. The marines sent him to Naval Aviation Cadet (NAVCAD) training, where he was commissioned. He and his wife, Nancy, had three children, Connie, Tony, and Pete.

He received the Distinguished Flying Cross for heroism and extraordinary aerial achievement. Wheeler was the world record holder for air hours as a flight instructor and was awarded seven medals for achievement in aerial flight, the Navy Achievement Medal for Outstanding Service, the Vietnamese Cross of Gallantry, and many other honors during his service.

Lacey served three tours of duty in Southeast Asia. He was shot down over Laos while on a reconnaissance mission on April 21, 1970. He and his copilot managed to parachute to the ground safely and call in for a helicopter rescue. The rescue team was able to get his copilot into the helicopter, but it came under heavy fire and had to leave Lacey. They were still in electronic communication with him for about a day after he was downed but could not recover him. His fate remains unknown.

They Paid the Cost of Freedom

Ohio's Small Town Museum has a flag that demonstrates the high cost of freedom. Service flags represent the sacrifice of local families during World War II. It is a sad reminder, and yet it is a source of immense pride that people from here met their duty to our country even until the end.

Here are the names of others who have given the last full measure of courage in service to our country:

Cpl. Richard Samuel Brown (KIA in Vietnam)

Pvt. John Caldwell (influenza during WWI)

Pvt. Chester Squire (pneumonia during WWI)

Pvt. Leslie Hill (KIA during the Aisne-Marne Offensive in WWI)

Pvt. Clarence Monroe Zwayer (pneumonia during WWI)

Pvt. John Henson (KIA near Paderborn, Germany, in WWII)

Endnotes

The Dog that Voted Republican. McNutt, Randy. *Lost Ohio*. Kent, OH: Kent State University Press, 2006, p. 142.

Pohlen, Jerome. *Oddball Ohio: A Guide to Some Really Strange Places*. Chicago, IL: Chicago Review Press, 2004, p. 186.

The Day Pigs Flew. "Majority Against Hanna." *New York Times* (New York, NY), January 4, 1898, p. 1.

The Rooster that Paid for His Own Meal. Darby, Erasmus Foster [David Webb]. *The Rooster King of Ashville, Ohio*. Chillicothe, OH: The Ohio Valley Folk Tale Research Project, Ross County Historical Society, 1955.

Hines, Robert L. "Chic-Chic, The Tale of a Rooster," in *Snake Den Surprise: Unearthing Ancient Secrets*. Lexington, KY: Ashville Area Heritage Society, 2017, pgs. 122-130.

The Debate Rages On. Pohlen, Jerome. "Why Chickens Are Smarter Than Dogs," in *Oddball Ohio: A Guide to Some Really Strange Places*. Chicago, IL: Chicago Review Press, 2004, p. 186.

No Michelangelo, But . . ."Freak Goose Egg." *Pickaway County News* (Ashville, OH), April 2, 1925, p. 1.

Kermit the Frog and the Puppetry Capital Latshaw, George. *The Complete Book of Puppetry*. Mineola, NY: Dover Publications, 1978, p. 145.

Puppeteers of America, Inc. *Code of Regulations*, Section 1. 2002.

"Puppeteers of America" [web page]. *Muppet Wiki*. Retrieved from https://muppet.fandom. com/wiki/Puppeteers_of_America.

Lifting the Veil of Economic Depression. "An Egg with Three Yolks—Something to Cackle About." *Pickaway County News* (Ashville, OH), August 13, 1931, p. 1.

"Eggstraordinary: NSW woman cracks open rare triple-yolk egg." *Sydney Morning Herald* (Sydney, Australia), January 1, 2019. Retrieved from https://www.smh.com.au/national/nsw/eggstraordinary-nsw-woman-cracks-open-rare-triple-yolk-egg-20190101-p50p52. html.

Clashing with Captain Kangaroo. Hines, Robert L. Correspondence with Gayle Anderson [notebook]. Ashville, OH: Ashville Area Heritage Society Library, 1998.

Butler, Kevin S. "Remembering Doug Anderson." Retrieved from http://www.tvparty.com/50-doug-anderson.html.

Anderson, Jock. "Remembering Doug Anderson." *Puppeteers of America*, v. 65, no. 3. (2014), p. 32.

Peacock Greeters. "Pair of Peacocks Call Pickaway County Post Office Home." WBNS-TV10 (Columbus, OH), July 19, 2012.

"2 Peacocks Roost at Post Office in Central Ohio" *Newsday* (New York, NY), July 20, 2012. Retrieved from https://www.newsday.com/news/nation/2-peacocks-roost-at-post-office-in-central-ohio-1.3851212.

Abdominal Snowman. Hines, Robert L. *Orient Inventors and their Patents* [exhibit]. Ashville, OH: Ashville Area Heritage Society Library, 2017.

The Original Spiderman. Bedini, Silvio. "Along Came a Spider—Spinning Silk for Cross-Hairs (The Search for Cross-Hairs for Scientific Instrumentation, Part II)." *The American Surveyor* (Frederick, MD), May 2005. Retrieved from http://archive.amerisurv.com/PDF/TheAmericanSurveyor_BediniAlongCameASpiderPart2_May2005.pdf.

"Spider Silk for Bomb Sights." *Flying* (Winter Park, FL), v. 31, no. 1 (July 1942), p. 62.

"He Works with Strands of Spider Silk." *Popular Science* (Harlan, IA), v. 133, n. 4. (October 1938), p. 80.

"Experts Lay Hindenburg Tragedy to Electrostatic or Backfire; One Theory Is That Airship Gathered Energy from Storm Which Caused Spark to Set Off Hydrogen; Another Is That Engine Ignited Gas; Lightning Flash Also Held a Possibility." *New York Times* (New York, NY), May 8, 1937, p. 1.

Fighting the Evil Weevil. Coleman, Lyle. "Thaddeus Hedges Parks, 1887–1971." *Journal of Economic Entomology*, v. 64, iss. 6. (December 1, 1971), p. 1578.

Goodness Snakes Alive. Hines, Robert L. *Snake Den Surprise: Unearthing Ancient Secrets.* Lexington, KY: Ashville Area Heritage Society, 2017, pgs. 55-59.

History of Franklin and Pickaway Counties, Ohio. Columbus, OH: Williams Brothers, 1880, p. 273.

Loving Nature–Even Snakes. "2017 Leadership in Philanthropy Award Winners—Dr. Louise (Omie) Warner and Clyde W. Gosnell, Jr." [web page]. *The Columbus Foundation.* Retrieved from https://columbusfoundation.org/stories-of-impact/2017-leadership-in-philanthropy-award-winners.

Soup of the Day–Coin Collector. "Finds Pennies in Turtle." *San Bernardino News* (San Bernardino, CA), July 19, 1915, p. 4.

"Finds Pennies in Turtle." *The Leaf Chronicle* (Clarksville, TN), September 30, 1915, p. 2.

"Finds Pennies in Turtle." *Webster City Freeman* (Webster City, IA), November 2, 1915, p. 2.

Moll, Don, and Edward O. Moll. *The Ecology, Exploitation and Conservation of River Turtles.* Cary, NC: Oxford University Press, 2004, p. 200.

Serving Turtle Soup Attractively. "Florence Brobeck, at 84, Food Writer and Editor." *New York Times* (New York, NY), March 11, 1979, p. 32.

Fraunfelter, Emmit, and John Shuemaker. *First Directory of the Village of Ashville.* Ashville, OH: Enterprise Publishing, 1896, p. 18.

Ashcraft, Kathryn Gorrell. "Outstanding Graduates," in *The Ohio State University School of Home Economics—A History 1896-1970.* Columbus, OH: The Ohio State University, 1970, p. 24.

The Great Pumpkin. Ebert, Ruth. "Coon Brothers." *Ashville Area Heritage Society Newsletter* (Ashville, OH), 2019, v. 20, n.1, pgs. 7-10.

Fun Guy with Fungi Humphrey, Harry Baker. "William Ashbrook Kellerman," in Makers of North American Botany. New York, NY: Ronald Press, 1961. Retrieved from https://siarchives.si.edu/collections/auth_per_fbr_eacp410

"Explorations in the Wild Interior of Guatemala by O.S.U. Men, Add Rich Treasures to the Stores of Science." Columbus, OH: *Columbus Dispatch*, April 1, 1906, Section 2, p. 1.

Over My Dead Body. Davis, Johnda. "South Bloomfield's Twin Elms." *Pickaway Quarterly* (Circleville, OH), Spring 1974, p. 10.

"Twin Elms Story." *Circleville Herald* (Circleville, OH), October 26, 1928, p. 2.

Big Tree Hunter. Cauchon, Dennis. "These Hunters Have Unusual Aim: Trees." *Courier-Post* (Camden, NJ), July 1, 2011, p. 1.

"Largest Sycamore Tree in the United States." Originally published in *Columbus Citizen* (Columbus, OH), [no date]. Retrieved from https://digital-collections.columbuslibrary.org/digital/collection/p16802coll7/id/8145/.

Shot Dead by a Mad Cow. "A Sad Accident," *Ashville Home News* (Ashville, OH), December 10, 1904, p. 3.

He Got the Green Light. "He Saved Others, Himself He Could Not Save." *Bulletin of the Montana Department of Public Health* (Helena, MT), June-July 1919, p. 5.

Lyz. "Green Light (1937)" [blog post], April 18, 2009. *And You Call Yourself a Scientist!?* Retrieved from http://www.aycyas.com/greenlight.htm.

The Great Blue Heron. "Great Blue Heron" [web page]. Retrieved from http://www.ohiobirds. org/obba2/pdfs/species/GreatBlueHeron.pdf.

I Voted. Kasler, Karen. "Teays Valley High School Senior Wins Voting Sticker Design Contest" [podcast], May 22, 2019, WOSU (Columbus, OH). Retrieved from https://radio.wosu. org/post/teays-valley-high-school-senior-wins-voting-sticker-design-contest#stream/0.

Ouch! "Hunting Mishap." *Pickaway County News* (Ashville, OH), October 13, 1916, p. 1.

Gun Barrel Diplomacy. Warner, Louise. "A Series of Articles Recounting the History of the Stratford Ecological Center and the Warner Family, Part 10: Gale's Marriage and Stratford's Beginnings" [web page]. *Stratford Ecological Center*. Retrieved from https:// stratfordecologicalcenter.org/legacy/.

Heritage, Timothy, and Catherine de Pury. "Tanks, Pies and Flowers; Resisting 1991 Soviet Coup" [web page]. *Reuters*, August 16, 2011. Retrieved from https://www.reuters.com/ article/us-russia-coup-protester/tanks-pies-and-flowers-resisting-1991-soviet-coup-idUSTRE77F2GE20110816.

He Got the Drop on Them. "He Played with Them." *Morning Call* (San Francisco, CA), October 13, 1890, p. 4.

Calaboose Calamity. "News Summary." *Daily Republican* (Wilmington, DE), September 28, 1883, p. 1.

Christie, J. Lute. "The Jail at Ashville, Ohio." *Superior Times* (Superior, WI), September 29, 1883, p. 2.

Cuffroth, A. B. "News of the Week." *The Tribune* (McCook, NE), October 4, 1883, p. 7.

"Horrible Affair at Ashville—The Calaboose and a Man Therein Burned." *Circleville Democrat and Watchman* (Circleville, OH), September 28, 1883, p. 3.

Encounter of the Third Kind. "Sighting Report" [web page]. *National UFO Reporting Center*, June 15, 1984. Retrieved from http://www.nuforc.org/webreports/035/S35723.html.

A Martian Invader Lived Here. Smith, P. H., et al. "H$_2$O at the Phoenix Landing Site." *Science*, v. 325, iss. 5936 (July 3, 2009), pgs. 58–61.

Niebur, Susan. "Diana Blaney: Play to Your Strengths" [blog post], September 24, 2010. *Women in Planetary Science*. Retrieved from https://womeninplanetaryscience.wordpress. com/2010/09/24/diana-blaney-play-to-your-strengths/.

Sleeping Beauty . . . Sort Of. Leatherwood, Gale. "The Stranger." *Ashville Area Heritage Society Newsletter* (Ashville, OH), v. 9, no. 1 (January 1, 2005), p. 5.

Go for It. Applegate, Jane. "SBA Awards Honors Best in the Business." *Indianapolis Star* (Indianapolis, IN), June 1, 1998, p. 25.

Vikings . . . Here? Mallery, Arlington H. *Lost America: The Story of Iron-Age Civilization Prior to Columbus*. Columbus, OH: The Overlook Company, 1951.

Hines, Robert L. *Snake Den Surprise: Unearthing Ancient Secrets*. Lexington, KY: Ashville Area Heritage Society, 2017, pgs. 103-104.

Viking Hoard Invades Ashville. Collins, Steven. "Another Huzzah for the Viking Fest." *Circleville Herald* (Circleville, OH), April 16, 2019, p. 1.

The Silver-Tongued Orator. "William Jennings Bryan to Speak at Chautauqua." *Pickaway County News* (Ashville, OH), August 2, 1918, p. 1.

The Speaker Has Spoken. Catledge, Turner. "Thunder in the Senate." *New York Times* (New York, NY), September 24, 1939, p. 113.

A Visit from the Devil. "Horned Toad." *Ashville Home News* (Ashville, OH), August 13, 1909, p. 3.

McDaniel, Tiffany. *The Summer that Melted Everything*. New York, NY: St. Martin's Press, 2016.

Paradise Lost, Connection Found. "A Guide to the Evert Mordecai Clark Papers, 1920–1957" [web page]. *Briscoe Center for American History, The University of Texas at Austin.* Retrieved from https://legacy.lib.utexas.edu/taro/utcah/03740/cah-03740.html.

Are They Ever Ashamed? Vita, Tricia. "More Photos from the Glory Days of the Sideshow Banner" [blog post], November 23, 2013. *Amusing the Zillion.* Retrieved from https://amusingthezillion.com/2013/11/23/more-photos-from-the-glory-days-of-the-sideshow-banner/.

You Ain't Seen Nothing Yet. "Local Businessmen Pleased with Outlay for Big Celebration." *Pickaway County News* (Ashville, OH), June 1929, p. 1.
"Stage Is All Set for the Big Celebration: 12,000 People Expected to Visit Ashville." *Pickaway County News* (Ashville, OH), July 3, 1930, p. 1.

Smile . . . You're on Candid Camera. Anderson, Sherwood. *Home Town (The Face of America).* New York, NY: Alliance Book Corporation, 1940.
Wallner, Susan, New Jersey Network, and Films for the Humanities & Sciences. *Ben Shahn: Passion for Justice* [video]. Princeton, NJ: Films for the Humanities and Sciences, 2002, 20 minutes, 51 seconds.

Documenting the Ashville Fourth of July Celebration. Hammel, Lisa. "In Ashville, Ohio July 4th Means Food, Parades and More Food." *New York Times* (New York, NY), July 5, 1967, p. 44.
Vitez, Michael. "It's a Grand Old Time." *Philadelphia Inquirer* (Philadelphia, PA), July 4, 2002, Sec. E, p. 1.

Little Chicago. "Bang! Boom! Little Chicago." *Pickaway County News* (Ashville, OH), August 28, 1930, p. 4.

Teetotalers and Bootleggers. "Still Found on Williams Farm." *Pickaway County News* (Ashville, OH), September 19, 1929, p. 1.

The General. "Ohio to Recall Civil War Event." *Circleville Herald* (Circleville, OH), April 11, 1962, p. 10.

Andrews' Raiders Monument. "Captain Thomas Taken Sunday—Former Superintendent of National Cemeteries Dead; Lived in Ashville." *Circleville Herald* (Circleville, OH), July 6, 1934, p. 1.

Moral Victory? Fullen, Larry. *The Broncos of 1945.* Bloomington, IN: AuthorHouse, 2010, pgs. 45–46.

We Also Kicked Butts. Hines, Robert L. *We Are . . .* [exhibit]. Ashville, OH: Ohio's Small Town Museum, 2019.

The "Blue Death" Cholera Cemetery. "Resolution 14-40—A Resolution to Approve the Excavation of the Harrison Township Cholera Cemetery . . . for Research Which Would be Done at The Ohio State University. A Request by Giuseppe Vercellotti, Professor." Harrison Township, OH: Harrison Township Trustees, May 20, 2014.

The Horror of Cholera. "Cholera Epidemics" [webpage]. *Ohio History Connection.* Retrieved from http://www.ohiohistorycentral.org/w/Cholera_Epidemics.

The Horror of Andersonville Prison. Clutters, Tom and Kathy, Eds. *Ohio Deaths in Confederate Prisons & Ohio Deaths on Steamer* Sultana. Ironton, OH: self-published, c. 1990, p. 14.
Hines, Robert L. "Pvt. Adam Beers and the Andersonville Prisoner of War Camp" [Facebook post], May 8, 2018. Retrieved from https://www.facebook.com/OhiosSmallTownMuseum/.
Cossean, Tony. "Pvt. Adam Beers" [web page]. Retrieved from https://www.findagrave.com/memorial/27403317/adam-beers.

World's Largest Woman (and Ghost). "Death of the Fat Woman of Ohio." *New York Times* (New York, NY), July 11, 1855, p. 1.

Powell, W. Byrd. "Mrs. Catharine Schooley, The Wonderfully Adipo-Lymphatic Lady." *Eclectic Medical Journal* (Cincinnati, OH), v. 5, no. 4. (April 1853), pgs. 163–170.

Martinelli, Patricia A., and Charles A. Stansfield Jr. *Haunted New Jersey: Ghosts and Strange Phenomena of the Garden State*. Mechanicsburg, PA: Stackpole Books, 2004, p. 77.

Headless Deaf Woman. Darst, Lillie C. "Woman Killed by Cars at Ashville." *Circleville Herald* (Circleville, OH), September 22, 1880, p. 4.

Screaming Mules at Stage's Pond. Quackenbush, Jannette Rae. *Ohio Ghost Hunter Guide V: A Haunted Hocking Ghost Hunter Guide*. 21 Crows Dusk to Dawn Publishing, 2013, p. 208.

You Can't Help but Scream. Allen, Michael. "*Cruel Will* Delivers a Violent Message: Release Details" [blog post], March 1, 2013. Retrieved from http://www.28dayslateranalysis.com/2013/03/cruel-will-delivers-violent-message.html.

When It Comes to Natural Disasters... Crawford, D. M. "Follows Film Career." *Circleville Herald* (Circleville, OH), March 15, 1986. p. 1.

Detached Body Part Burials. Lore, David. "Ohio Prehistoric Graves Continue to Astonish Archaeologists" [blog post], September 9, 2001. *Columbus Dispatch* (Columbus, OH). Retrieved from https://rense.com/general14/sassad.htm.

Skeleton in the Attic. "Skeleton: Found in the Attic of a South Bloomfield Home Causes Excitement." *Ashville Home News* (Ashville, OH), April 29, 1905, p. 2.

The Great Tribute. Hines, Robert L. *Snake Den Surprise: Unearthing Ancient Secrets*. Lexington, KY: Ashville Area Heritage Society, 2017, pgs. 8-10.

The Great Geologist. Berg, Thomas M. "John A. Bownocker" [PDF]. Retrieved from https://www.stategeologists.org/sites/default/files/remembrance/John-A-Bownocker-1865-1928.pdf.

Facedown Burial. Moorehead, Warren King, Ed. "Report of Field Work in Various Portions of Ohio." *Ohio Archaeological and Historical Society Quarterly Publication* (Columbus, OH), v. 7 (1897), p. 115.

Face Down a Mob. "Tributes to the Memory of Samuel Ritter Peters." *Newton Evening Kansas Republican* (Newton, KS), April 25, 1910, pgs. 2, 8.

When Life Gives You Formaldehyde. Hines, Robert L., and Charles Morrison. "Dr. Chester Rockey Talking about Early Ashville" [tape recording]. Recorded in Ashville, OH, October 23, 1978.

Paraskevidekatriaphobia -13. Adams, Cecil. "The Straight Dope" [blog post], November 5, 1992. Retrieved from https://www.chicagoreader.com/chicago/the-straight-dope/Content?oid=880773.

The Contrarian. Hafey, Luther. "George W. Brown." *Ashville Area Heritage Society Newsletter* (Ashville, OH), February 1, 2018, p. 3.

Death of an Era? Hines, Robert L. "The Quilt." *Ashville Area Heritage Society Newsletter* (Ashville, OH), January 2010, p. 1.

Stopping Traffic. "Teddy Boor Receives Patent for Cornering Plow." *Circleville Herald* (Circleville, OH), February 5, 1940, p. 3.

Guinness World Records, Limited. "World's Oldest Functional Traffic Signal," in *Guinness World Records 2018*. New York, NY: Bantam Books, 2017, p. 212.

Not the First Traffic Light. Bellis, Mary. "The History of Roads and Asphalt" [web page]. Retrieved from http://theinventors.org/library/inventors/blasphalt.htm.

I Will Sign My Own Name. Amram, Fred. "The Innovative Woman." *New Scientist* (London, UK), v. 102, no. 1411 (May 1984), p. 10.

Hines, Robert L. "Inventor Eliza Steward" [Facebook post], April 26, 2018. Retrieved from https://www.facebook.com/OhiosSmallTownMuseum/.

United States Patent and Trademark Office, March 27, 1900. Apparel Corset, Patent #646,082.

United States Patent and Trademark Office, August 29, 1899. Device for Stretching Table Cloths, Patent #632,159.

Other Female Firsts. "Gretchen Anne Hedges Srigley Seitsinger." *Ashville Area Heritage Society Newsletter* (Ashville, OH), v. 14, no. 1 (February 1, 2011), p. 3.

Office of Press Secretary. "President Clinton Names Nikki Rush Tinsley as Inspector General at the Environmental Protection Agency" [press release], April 23, 1988. Washington, DC: The White House.

Barnes, Joey. "Fisher Takes Pride in Helping Put Newgarden on Title Path" [blog post], September 25, 2017. Retrieved from https://www.indycar.com/News/2017/09/09-25-Fisher-on-Newgarden.

Ashcraft, Kathryn Gorrell. "Outstanding Graduates," in *The Ohio State University School of Home Economics—A History 1896-1970.* Columbus, OH: The Ohio State University, 1970, p. 24.

"Diana Blaney: MER Deputy Project Scientist" [web page]. Retrieved from https://science.jpl.nasa.gov/people/Blaney/.

Knapp, Caroline. "Last Words." *New York Times* (New York, NY), June 28, 1998, Sec. 7, p. 21.

Latshaw, George. *The Complete Book of Puppetry.* Mineola, NY: Dover Publications, 1978, p. 145.

Staff (*Christian Century*). "Mary Hinkle Shore Becomes Rector and Dean of ELCA Seminary in Southeast" [blog post], March 20, 2019. Retrieved from https://www.christiancentury.org/article/people/mary-hinkle-shore-becomes-rector-and-dean-elca-seminary-southeast.

Poo-Powered Batteries. United States Patent and Trademark Office, December 30, 1997. Sewage Sludge Composite Battery, Patent #5,702,835.

Everybody Has to Start Somewhere. "Ross Larue, PhD" [web page]. *The Ohio State University College of Pharmacy* (Columbus, OH). Retrieved from https://pharmacy.osu.edu/directory/ross-larue.

Look Away, He's Gonna Jump! United States Patent and Trademark Office, September 3, 1907. Fire Escape Device, Patent #865,167A.

Boyer, Clarence. "An Ingenious Invention." *Pickaway Quarterly* (Circleville, OH), Summer 2013, p. 10.

Filter Out Any Distractions. "About Us" [web page]. *Columbus Industries, Inc.* Retrieved from https://www.colind.com/about-us/.

What Is the Capital of Bolivia? Hines, Robert L. "Eye-Que: Fun and Educational." *Ashville Area Heritage Society Newsletter* (Ashville, OH), v. 6., no. 1 (January 1, 2002), p. 6.

Higher Education. Bowers, G. Robert. "Harold Jennings Bowers, a Son's Perspective." *Pickaway Quarterly* (Circleville, OH), Fall 2008, pgs. 14–20.

Driverless Car. "Seven New Teachers Hired at Teays Valley; Resignations Read." *Pickaway County News* (Ashville, OH), July 7, 1966, p. 1.

Hartford, Bill. "You 'Fly' This Car with a Stick." *Popular Mechanics* (New York, NY), April 1967, pgs. 87–89, 207.

Ackerman, Evan. "The Electronic Highway. How 1960s Visionaries Presaged Today's Autonomous Vehicles" [blog post], August 2, 2016. *IEEE Spectrum.* Retrieved from https://spectrum.ieee.org/cars-that-think/transportation/self-driving/the-electronic-highway-of-1969.

Fenton, Robert E., and Karl W. Olson. "The Electronic Highway." *IEEE Spectrum*, v. 6, iss. 7 (July 1969), pgs. 60–66.

On Every Street and Down Every Country Road. Hines, Robert L. "A Listing of Patented Inventors from the Teays Valley School District Area." Ashville, OH: Ohio's Small Town Museum Library, 2017.

On Paper, It Will Fly. "Big Airship Being Built: St. Louis Man Has Invented a New Type to Carry 100 Passengers." *New York Times* (New York, NY), July 7, 1910, p. 1.
"Invents Airship to Carry Scores: St Louis Man Constructs Machine to Upset All Laws of Gravity." *Washington Times* (Washington, DC), July 7, 1910, p. 11.
"Plans Immense Airship: St. Louis Man Expects to Carry 100 Men at 100 Miles an Hour." *New York Tribune* (New York, NY), July 7, 1910, p. 1.

Sifting Moon Dust. "Charles W. Ward, Inventor of the Sonic Sifter." *Allen-Bradley Horizons Magazine*, No. 2 (1989), pgs. 20–21.

Occupation: Outlaw. US Bureau of Census, 1880. Scioto Township, Thomas McDonald.
"Traced to a Tree—Judge Lynch Holds Court in Ohio—The Body of a Bully Found Dangling in Mid-Air." *St. Louis Globe Democrat* (St. Louis, MO), September 2, 1880, p. 1.
"Ohio Ku-Klux—Damnable Deed in Pickaway County." *Hocking Sentinel* (Logan, OH), September 9, 1880, p. 1.

Hanging at Main and Long. "World War Ended—Germany Signed the Allies' Armistice Peace Terms Monday Morning at Midnight. Overjoyed Citizens Celebrated." *Pickaway County News* (Ashville, OH), November 15, 1918, p. 1.

Nobody's Perfect, Your Honor. "Monologue." *The Tonight Show Starring Johnny Carson.* Burbank, CA: NBC, April 1980.
Swierczynski, Duane. "#227. Earl Ellery Wright—Bank Robber," in *The Encyclopedia of the FBI's Ten Most Wanted List: Over Fifty Years of Convicts, Robbers, Terrorists, and Other Rogues.* New York, NY: Skyhorse Publishing, 2014, p. 138.
"Bank Robber Sent to Prison." *Akron Beacon Journal* (Akron, OH), April 24, 1980, p. 25.
"Most Wanted Robber Nabbed in City Motel." *Coshocton Tribune* (Coshocton, OH), June 21, 1966, p. 4.

A Match Cover Did Him In. Focht, Carolyn. "Ashville Marshal Wins Wide Praise—License Jotting Led to Bank Robber." *Columbus Dispatch* (Columbus, OH), November 21, 1965, p. 33A.

Perfect Attendance. Holden, Stephen. "One Actor's Particular, Um, Talent." *New York Times* (New York, NY), January 12, 2001, Sec. E, p. 39.

Dr. Hosler's Starring Role. "Doctor for Indigent Sick." *Pickaway County News* (Ashville, OH), March 7, 1929, p. 1.
"Ashville Physician Dies at 89." *Circleville Herald* (Circleville, OH), May 22, 1978, p. 1.

C'mon Now, We Have All Done Something Stupid. Christie, Joel. "Are These the Dumbest Thieves Ever? Cocky Bank Robbing Couple Arrested 'After Posing for Facebook Photos with the Thousands of Dollars Cash They Stole'" [web page]. *Daily Mail* (London, UK), September 24, 2015. Retrieved from https://www.dailymail.co.uk/news/article-3248275/Are-dumbest-thieves-Cocky-bank-robbing-couple-arrested-posing-Facebook-photos-thousands-dollars-cash-stole.html.

Not Many of Us Do Something This Smart. "Richard Valentine Baum." *Arizona Republic* (Phoenix, AZ), March 22, 2015, p. F8.
Wiley, Carl A. "Synthetic Aperture Radars—A Paradigm for Technology Evolution." *IEEE Transactions on Aerospace and Electronic Systems*, v. 21, no. 3 (May 1985), p. 441.

Wait a Minute, What? Lewin, Tamar. "Custody Case in Ohio Ends in Slaying and Prison Term." *New York Times* (New York, NY), December 8, 1990, Sec. 1, p. 9.

The End of Polygamy. Carter, Joe. "9 Things You Should Know about Surrogacy" [blog post], June 6, 2014. *The Gospel Coalition.* Retrieved from https://www.thegospelcoalition.org/article/9-things-you-should-know-about-surrogacy/.
Whitney, Orson F. "The Dark Before the Dawn (1886–1887)," in *Popular History of Utah.* Salt Lake City, UT: The Deseret News, 1916, pgs. 449–452.
"Remarks Made by President Wilford Woodruff." *Deseret Evening News* (Salt Lake City, UT), November 7, 1891, p. 4.

Woodruff, Wilford. "Official Declaration 1," October 6, 1890. *The Church of Jesus Christ of Latter-Day Saints*. Retrieved from https://www.churchofjesuschrist.org/study/scriptures/dc-testament/od/1?lang=eng.

Don't Drink the Water. Fridley, Steve. "Ability Sought—The Standard Chemical Company, the World's Largest Producer of Radium Secures the Services of H. M. Plum." *Pickaway County News* (Ashville, OH), June 21, 1918, p. 1.

Plum, H. M. "The Extraction and Separation of the Radioactive Constituents of Carnotite." *Journal of the American Chemical Society* (Washington, DC), v. 37, no. 8 (August 1915), pgs. 1797–1816.

Fridley, Steve. "Visits Radium Mines—Dr. H. M. Plum in Mountain Wilds of Colorado as Chemical Expert for the Standard Chemical Company of Pittsburgh, PA." *Pickaway County News* (Ashville, OH), November 25, 1920, p. 1.

"1921: Marie Curie Visits the US" [web page], August 13, 2009, upd. September 26, 2016. *National Institute of Standards and Technology, Physical Measurement Laboratory*. Retrieved from https://www.nist.gov/pml/1921-marie-curie-visits-us.

High-Level Nuclear Waste *Community Development Handbook*. Columbus, OH: Battelle Memorial Institute Office of Nuclear Waste Isolation, 1982.

Liquid Poison. *A Brief History of Pickaway County, to Accompany Wheeler's Map*. Circleville, OH: Scott and Teesdale's Power Press, 1844, p. 17.

National Liquor Company. "National Liquor Company" [advertisement]. *Ashville Home News* (Ashville, OH), March 30, 1907, p. 5.

The Rowdiest Bar in America? "Ohio Firefighters Respond to Blaze" [blog post], April 19, 2008. *Firehouse*. Retrieved from https://www.firehouse.com/photo-story/article/10566853/ohio-firefighters-respond-to-blaze.

"Pickaway County Icon Burns" [web page]. *Columbus Dispatch* (Columbus, OH), April 30, 2008. Retrieved from https://www.dispatch.com/content/stories/local/2008/04/30/Stagecoach.ART_ART_04-30-08_B3_UHA2N4S.html.

Pioneer Recording Artist. "Chart Results for Corrine Morgan" [web page]. *Playback FM*. Retrieved from https://playback.fm/search?c=chart_post&s=corrine+morgan.

"Corinne Morgan (vocalist: contralto)" [web page]. *Discography of American Historical Records*. Retrieved from https://adp.library.ucsb.edu/index.php/talent/detail/41046/Morgan_Corinne_vocalist_contralto.

Silver Surprise. "Prehistoric Bones—Nuggets of Silver and Human Skeletons in Ohio Mounds." *Salt Lake Herald* (Salt Lake City, UT), June 27, 1897, p. 10.

Hines, Robert L. *Snake Den Surprise: Unearthing Ancient Secrets*. Lexington, KY: Ashville Area Heritage Society, 2017, pgs. 23-28.

Search for Missing Silver Nuggets. Hines, Robert L. *Snake Den Surprise: Unearthing Ancient Secrets*. Lexington, KY: Ashville Area Heritage Society, 2017, pgs. 32-33.

Landlocked Naval Commanders. "Captain Christy." *Pickaway County News* (Ashville, OH), December 18, 1918, p. 1.

"The *San Diego*, Sunk Off Long Island." *New York Times* (New York, NY), July 20, 1918, p. 1.

"Captain H. H. Christy Promoted to Admiral." *Pickaway County News* (Ashville, OH), January 15, 1925, p. 1.

"NBAA Honors Doswell Award Winner, Local Committee Chair and 5 Year Safe Flying Achievement Award Winners" [press release], Oct. 12, 2000. *National Business Aviation Association*. Retrieved from https://nbaa.org/uncategorized/nbaa-honors-doswell-award-winner-local-committee-chair-and-50-year-safe-flying-achievement-award-winners/.

Landlocked Oceanographers. Martin, Cassie. "For the Love of Physics" [blog post], December 17, 2015. *Earth, Atmospheric and Planetary Sciences (EAPS)*. Retrieved from https://eapsweb.mit.edu/news/2015/for-the-love-of-physics.

Baum, Steven K. *Glossary of Physical Oceanography and Related Disciplines*. College Station, TX: Texas A&M University, 2004.

Which Way Is North? "Traction Depot Reversed." *Ashville Home News* (Ashville, OH), September 9, 1905, p. 2.

Black Jack Pershing Is Heading North Ohio-Midland Power and Light Company. *Highlights of Our First Half Century*. Canal Winchester, OH: Ohio-Midland Power and Light Company, 1949, p. 7.
Pershing, John J. *John J. Pershing Diary*. Set 5, July 31, 1919–July 11, 1920 [diary], pgs. 62–63. Held at Library of Congress, *John J. Pershing Papers, 1882–1971*. Retrieved from https://www.wdl.org/en/item/18494/.

A Token of My Love. Baum, John. "History of Duvall, 1860–1969." *Pickaway Quarterly* (Circleville, OH), Winter 1970, pgs. 6-10.

Buckeye Blacksmith. Bear, John W. *The Life and Travels of John W. Bear, "the Buckeye Blacksmith."* Baltimore, MD: Binswanger and Company, 1879, pgs. 233–234.
Snay, Mitchell. *Horace Greeley and the Politics of Reform in Nineteenth-Century America*. Lanham, MD: Bowman and Littlefield, 2011, p. 21.

Perplexing Parallel and Right-Angle Pits. Hines, Robert L. *Snake Den Surprise: Unearthing Ancient Secrets*. Lexington, KY: Ashville Area Heritage Society, 2017, p. 54.

Learning More about the Daily Lives of the Ancient Hopewell. "Adventures in Paleoethnobotany with Dr. DeeAnne Wymer" [podcast], December 19, 2018. Night-Light Radio. Retrieved from https://www.buzzsprout.com/56282/895271.
Hines, Robert L. *Snake Den Surprise: Unearthing Ancient Secrets*. Lexington, KY: Ashville Area Heritage Society, 2017, pgs. 80-95.

Hey, That Sounds Like a Great Idea! "Aerial Bomb Exploding at 4:00" [advertisement]. *Pickaway County News* (Ashville, OH), June 29, 1961, p. 2.
Auble, John, Jr. "Believe It or Not: It Was Too Much of a Blast at Ashville." *Citizen-Journal* (Columbus, OH), July [unknown], 1961.

Really Great Business Ideas. "Promoting Service and Leadership, The Harold I. Richard Scholarship," in *The Ohio State University Foundation 2010 Annual Report*. Columbus, OH: The Ohio State University, 2010.
"Floyd Edwin Younkin." *Palm Beach Post* (Palm Beach, FL), July 23, 1997, p. 16.

Optical Illusion? Mele, Andrew. *Tearin' Up the Pea Patch: the Brooklyn Dodgers, 1953*. Jefferson, NC: McFarland, 2015, p. 77.
"Baseball's Curve Balls—Are They Optical Illusions?" *Life* (New York, NY), September 15, 1941, p. 83.
"Feller Curve No Trick of Eye, Physicist Says." *New York Daily News* (New York, NY), September 26, 1941, p. 68.

Life Magazine Cover. Silk, George. Cover image. *Life* (New York, NY), April 5, 1948.
Blackledge, Steve. "Brush with Greatness." *Columbus Dispatch* (Columbus, OH), July 19, 2007, p. 01C.

Hearty Stock. "Supt. J. H. Sark Had Accidents—Fell Down Elevator Shaft At Crites Canning Factory In Ashville." *Pickaway County News* (Ashville, OH), June 7, 1923, p. 2.

In Good Running Shape. Freeburg, Nathan. "The Only Three Things You Need to Know about Running: A Conversation with Mark Remy" [podcast], February 23, 2017. *Brewery Running Series*. Retrieved from https://breweryrunningseries.com/2017/02/conversation-with-mark-remy/.

Bitter Rivals. Hines, Robert L. "Nobody Won!" *Ashville Area Heritage Society Newsletter* (Ashville, OH), January 1, 2016, p. 4.

Time Ran Out-or Did It? Hornung, Paul. "Bucks Lose to MSU in Wild Finish." *Columbus Dispatch* (Columbus, OH), November 10, 1974, p. E-1.
Natali, Alan. "Harold 'Champ' Henson," in *Woody's Boys: 20 Famous Buckeyes Talk Amongst Themselves*. Wilmington, OH: Orange Frazer Press, 1995, pgs. 209-230.

Dancing with the Star. Van Cleaf, Aaron R. *History of Pickaway County, Ohio and Representative Citizens.* Chicago, IL: Biographical Publishing Company, 1906, p. 174.

MacDonald, Hugh. "Getting to the Heart of Burns with Robert McCroskie" [web page]. *National.* January 7, 2018. Retrieved from https://www.thenational.scot/news/15811944. getting-to-the-heart-of-burns-with-robert-mccroskie/.

Teen Dance-O-Rama. Meyers, David, Arnett Howard, James Loeffler, and Candice Watkins. *Columbus: The Musical Crossroads (Images of America).* Charleston, SC: Arcadia Publishing, 2008, p. 107.

"Teen Dance-O-Rama." *Billboard* (Cincinnati, OH), August 13, 1963, p. 42.

Seventeen Stars–Ohio's Oldest Flag. "Seventeen-Star Flag Displayed at Ohio's Bicentennial Celebration." *Flagwaver: Journal of Great Waters Association of Vexillology*, v. 8, no. 1 (May 2003). Retrieved from http://gwav.tripod.com/issue_15.htm.

The Siege of Detroit. Williams Bros. *History of Franklin and Pickaway Counties, Ohio: With Illustrations and Biographical Sketches of Some of the Prominent Men and Pioneers.* Cleveland, OH: Williams Bros., 1880, p. 347.

"Correspondence of Col. James Denny, of Circleville, OH. 1812–1815." *"Old Northwest" Genealogical Quarterly*, v. 10, no. 4 (October 1907), p. 292.

Accidental Munchkin "Hulse Youth Leaves For Kansas City to Join Midget Troupe." *Circleville Herald* (Circleville, OH), November 7, 1938, p. 1.

"Hulse Youth Among 130 to be in Movie." *Circleville Herald* (Circleville, OH), November 23, 1938, p. 2.

"Hulse Youth Returns After Work in Film." *Circleville Herald* (Circleville, OH), January 11, 1939, p. 2.

Other Top 100 American Films. "History News: Daniel Kellerman Selected to LCHS Hall of Fame." *Linn County News* (Pleasanton, KS), December 13, [unknown].

"Charlie Kearns." *IMDb.* Retrieved from https://www.imdb.com/name/nm0443989/?ref_=fn_al_nm_1.

To Hell with Protocols. "The People Arrive for Carter's Big Party." *Indianapolis Star* (Indianapolis, IN), January 20, 1977, p. 15.

"Billy Carter Gets His Way." *Times Herald-Record* (Middletown, NY), January 16, 1977, p. 2.

If Only They Had Followed Fire Safety Protocols. Brennan, Jack. "Even after 40 Years, It Feels Like the Beverly Hills Supper Club Fire Happened 'Last Night': An Oral History" [web page]. *WCPO*, May 22, 2017. Retrieved from https://www.wcpo.com/longform/the-beverly-hills-supper-club-fire-on-its-40th-anniversary-cincinnati-area.

"John B. Beaver." *Circleville Herald* (Circleville, OH), June 2, 1977, p. 2.

Al Capone and Ashville's Commodore Stoltz. Harris, Ginger. "Mondrian South Beach Hotel." *South Beach Magazine* (Miami Beach, FL), May 7, 2014. Retrieved from https://www.southbeachmagazine.com/mondrian-south-beach/.

North, Sam. "Miami—A Wonderful Invention" [blog post], 2001. Retrieved from https://www.hackwriters.com/Miami.htm.

Witness to a Mobster Murder. "Taylor Delays Bringing Coast Guards to Book—Solicitor Fails to Get Alleged Shannon Slayers on Docket." *Miami Daily News* (Miami, FL), May 2, 1927, p. M-3.

Mistaken Birthplace. Bellamy, John Stark, II. "Sarah Victor Scandal, 1868," in *Women Behaving Badly—True Tales of Cleveland's Most Ferocious Female Killers.* Cleveland, OH: Gray and Company, 2005, pgs. 157–190.

Victor, Sarah Marie. *The Life Story of Sarah M. Victor for Sixty Years: Convicted of Murdering Her Brother, Sentenced to be Hung, Had Sentence Commuted, Passed Nineteen Years in Prison, Yet Is Innocent.* Columbus, OH: The Williams Publishing Company, 1887.

Supreme Court of Ohio. "Commutation of Punishment for Crime Valid Without Acceptance by Convict—In the Matter of Sarah M. Victor." *Albany Law Journal* (Albany, NY), v. 17 (1878), p. 424.

"The Cleveland Tragedy: Conviction of Mrs. Victor for Poisoning Her Brother—Her Past Life—Circumstances of the Crime—Exciting Scenes in Court." *New York Times* (New York, NY), June 27, 1868, p. 1.

There Are Other Authors. Hines, Robert L. "A Listing of Ashville Area Authors." Ashville, OH: Ohio's Small Town Museum Library, 2019.

Mistaken Identity. "Rogers Pleads Not Guilty." *Pickaway County News* (Ashville, OH), April 11, 1929, p. 1.

Where, Oh Where, Are You Tonight? "'Phfft! You Were Gone': King 78" [blog post], April 28, 2016. *Zero to 180—Three Minute Magic: Discoveries of a Pop Music Archaeologist.* Retrieved from https://www.zeroto180.org/?p=23560.
Fox, Jon Hartley. *King of the Queen City: The Story of King Records.* Urbana, IL: University of Illinois Press, 2009, p. 43.

Untrue Love Will Find a Way. "Sweethearts Over 70 Years." *Western News* (Stevensville, MT), October 3, 1901, p. 6.
"Were Lovers for 71 Years.; An Old Couple in Ohio Finally Decide to Get Married." *New York Times* (New York, NY), May 28, 1900, p. 2.

Find a Way to Love Your Community. "Scholarships" [web page]. *Teays Valley Local Schools.* Retrieved http://www.tvsd.us/Scholarships.aspx

Solve This. Lucks, Barbara. "True Stories Told Live" [live event]. Broad Street Presbyterian Church (Columbus, OH), April 28, 2017.

Ashville's Atticus Finch and New Jerusalem. Stoker, G. B. "Voters Make Changes in Our Village Officials—Harry Margulis Elected Mayor." *Pickaway County News* (Ashville, OH), November 7, 1935, p. 1.

Make the Chicago River Flow Backward. Randolph, Isham. *Gleanings from a Harvest of Memories.* Columbia, MO: E.W. Stephens Company, 1937.
"Opening of the Chicago Drainage Canal." *Engineering News Record and American Railway Journal* (New York, NY), v. 43, no. 2 (January 11, 1900), p. 22.

Stand by Your Convictions. Rogers, J. David. "The American Engineers that Built the Panama Canal," in Bernard G. Dennis Jr., Ed., *Engineering the Panama Canal: A Centennial Retrospective: Proceedings of Sessions Honoring the 100th Anniversary of the Panama Canal at the ASCE Global Engineering Conference 2014, October 7–11, 2014, Panama City, Panama.* Reston, VA: American Society of Engineers, 2014, p. 84.
Hines, Robert L. "Randolph Street Mystery Solved." *Ashville Area Heritage Society Newsletter* (Ashville, OH), February 2012, p. 4.

Bring About Racial Equality. "General Benjamin Oliver Davis Jr." [web page]. *US Air Force.* Retrieved from https://www.af.mil/About-Us/Biographies/Display/Article/107298/general-benjamin-oliver-davis-jr/.

Pearl Farrow's War. "Another Name." *Circleville Union Herald* (Circleville, OH), December 19, 1918, p. 1.
Hines, Robert. L. "WWI Pvt. Pearl T. Farrow" [Facebook post], May 27, 2018. Retrieved from https://www.facebook.com/OhiosSmallTownMuseum/.

Make Spain Declare War on the United States. White, Trumbull. *Pictorial History of Our War with Spain for Cuba's Freedom.* Chicago, IL: Monarch Book Company, 1898, pgs. 31–32.

We Need to Declare Peace. "Departure of President Wilson for Europe—Members of Peace Delegation." *The Commercial and Financial Chronicle* (New York, NY), v. 107, no. 2 (December 7, 1918), p. 2143.

Did We Need to Imprison the Guiltless? Inomata, Kinji. *Pure Winds Bright Moon.* Los Angeles, CA: Stately Steward Publications, 2012.

Find an Indy 500 Sponsor. Boyle, Robert H. "Hot Pace in a Big Mini-Race." *Sports Illustrated* (New York, NY), December 7, 1970, p. 38.

What's After Winning? "Small Business Spotlight: Cook's Creek Golf Club [blog post], July 31, 2018. *VCNB Family*. Retrieved from https://vcnbfamily.me/tag/cooks-creek-golf-club/.

Bring More Excitement to Indy Racing. NWBC Council. "Sarah Fisher Appointed to National Women's Business Council" [press release], May 12, 2011. Retrieved from https://www.nwbc.gov/2011/05/12/sarah-fisher-appointed-to-national-womens-business-council/.

Karting Classic. *Commercial Point Karting Classic* [website]. Retrieved from http://cpkartingclassic.com/.

Commercial Point Homecoming *Commercial Point Community Men's Club Foundation* [Facebook page]. Retrieved from https://www.facebook.com/commercialpointcommunitymensclub/.

The Battle of Adobe Walls. Historical Society of New Mexico. *The California Column: Its Campaigns and Services in New Mexico, Arizona and Texas, during the Civil War.* Santa Fe, NM: New Mexican Printing Co., 1908, p. 36.
Miller, Charles C. *History of Fairfield County, Ohio and Representative Citizens.* Chicago, IL: Richmond-Arnold Publishing Co., 1912, p. 584.

Wounded Knee Massacre. Gill, Jeff. "Warren King Moorehead at Wounded Knee" [blog post], December 29, 2011. *Ohio History Connection*. Retrieved from https://www.ohiohistory.org/learn/collections/archaeology/archaeology-blog/2011/december-2011/warren-king-moorehead-at-wounded-knee.

Fleeing Slavery. Garst, Henry. *Otterbein University, 1847–1907.* Dayton, OH: United Brethren Publishing House; W. R. Funk, 1907.
"Our History" [web page]. *United Brethren*. Retrieved from https://ub.org/about/history/.

Dichotomy. "Walter Stewart" [web page]. *Owl Sports*. Retrieved from https://owlsports.com/coaches.aspx?rc=2189.

Viva la Revolución? "Major John Thomas Is to Be Fitted Out With a New Home by Uncle Sam." *Ashville Home News* (Ashville, OH), March 5, 1905, p. 1.
Thomas, John H. "John Writes Home." *Ashville Home News* (Ashville, OH), March 24, 1911, p. 1.

The Manifest Destiny War. "House Vote #223 in 1846 (29th Congress): To Concur in a Senate Amendment to H.R. 145 (16-9 Stat. 9, May 13, 1846), a Bill for the Prosecution of the War with Mexico by Eliminating a Clause Relating to Paying Volunteer Mounted Corps for the Use and Risk of Their Horses." *GovTrack*. Retrieved from https://www.govtrack.us/congress/votes#session=75&chamber[]=2.
"Perrill, Augustus Leonard" [web page]. *Biographical Directory of the United States Congress, 1774–Present*. Retrieved from http://bioguide.congress.gov/scripts/biodisplay.pl?index=P000240 .

9-11 Attack on the Pentagon. Wallace, Alan. "Actual Account of Fire-Fighter Alan Wallace" [PDF]. Retrieved from http://www.heartofamericaquilt.org/files/alanwallace.pdf.

Planting Corn at the Pentagon. Hallauer, Arnel R., Ed. *Specialty Corns*, 2nd ed. Boca Raton, FL: CRC Press, 2002, p. 401.
"Frederick D. Richey 1947–1954" [PDF]. *UTIA: Institute of Agriculture, The University of Tennessee*. Retrieved from https://ag.tennessee.edu/plantsciences/Documents/RetireeBiographies/FrederickRicheyBio.pdf.
Hines, Robert L. "Head of USDA Crop Services—Frederick Richey." *Ashville Area Heritage Society Newsletter* (Ashville, OH), January 1, 2003, p. 18.

Saving Captain Phillips. Phillips, Richard, with Stephan Talty. *A Captain's Duty: Somali Pirates, Navy SEALs,* and *Dangerous Days at Sea.* New York, NY: Hyperion, 2010, pgs. 274-275.
Bennett, Trish. "On the Front Lines: Ashville Man Sees Pirate Incident Up Close." *Circleville Herald* (Circleville, OH), April 24, 2009, pgs. A1, A3.

Can I Have Lobster? Kurtzman, Lori. "Woman Reunites with Firefighter Who Saved Her from Drowning." *Columbus Dispatch* (Columbus, OH), July 2, 2014, upd. July 3, 2014. Retrieved from https://www.dispatch.com/content/stories/local/2014/07/02/meeting-her-lifesaver.html

D-Day Invasion. 16th Infantry Regiment. *16th Infantry Regiment Roll of Honor: Regimental Casualties 1861–Present* [PDF], last updated February 12, 2017. Retrieved from http://16thinfassn.org/wp-content/uploads/2017/02/16th-Infantry-Roll-of-Honor-2017-02-12.pdf, p. 48.
Hines, Robert L. "WWII Pvt. William Schlarp" [Facebook post], May 22, 2018. Retrieved from https://www.facebook.com/OhiosSmallTownMuseum/.

Battle of the Bulge. Hines, Robert L. "WWII Pvt. Grant E. Puckett" [Facebook post], May 23, 2018. Retrieved from https://www.facebook.com/OhiosSmallTownMuseum/.
Hines, Robert L. "WWII Pvt. William Frederick Hinton" [Facebook post], May 18, 2018. Retrieved from https://www.facebook.com/OhiosSmallTownMuseum/.

Hürtgen Forest Battle. Hines, Robert L. "WWII Pvt. Jarold Roese" [Facebook post], May 20, 2018. Retrieved from https://www.facebook.com/OhiosSmallTownMuseum/.

Battle for Cassino. Hines, Robert L. "WWII Sgt. Earl A. White" [Facebook post], May 17, 2018. Retrieved from https://www.facebook.com/OhiosSmallTownMuseum/.

Battle of Iwo Jima. Smith, Larry. *Iwo Jima: World War II Veterans Remember the Greatest Battle of the Pacific.* New York, NY: W. W. Norton & Company, 2008.
"Iwo: D+10. March 1, 1945: Meatgrinder" [web page]. *First Battalion, 24th Marines: The History of the Men of 1/24 in World War II and Beyond.* Retrieved from https://1stbattalion24thmarines.com/the-battles/iwo-jima/d10/.

Air Losses. 1st Lt. Charles W. Mayberry
Hines, Robert L. "WWII Lt. Charles W. Mayberry" [Facebook post], May 19, 2018. Retrieved from https://www.facebook.com/OhiosSmallTownMuseum/.
Hines, Robert L. "WWII Lt. Richard A. Hedges" [Facebook post], May 16, 2018. Retrieved from https://www.facebook.com/OhiosSmallTownMuseum/.

Jellico Train Disaster. Hines, Robert L. "WWII Pvt. John R. Wickline and Pvt. Robert Prindle" [Facebook post], May 17, 2018. Retrieved from https://www.facebook.com/OhiosSmallTownMuseum

High-Priority Vietnam MIA/POW. Family Troubled by U.S. Actions after Pilot Went Down---Maj. Eugene Wheeler of Ashville, Who Disappeared in 1970, Is among 55 High Priority Cases the Pentagon Wants Resolved." *Columbus Dispatch* (Columbus, OH), p. 03D.

They Paid the Cost of Freedom. "Ashville Soldier Killed in Vietnam." *Circleville Herald* (Circleville, OH), July 13, 1968, p. 1.
"Five Sons of Pickaway County Dead." *Circleville Herald* (Circleville, OH), November 28, 1918, p. 1.

Appendix

Maps Showing the Intersection of Weird and Wonderful.

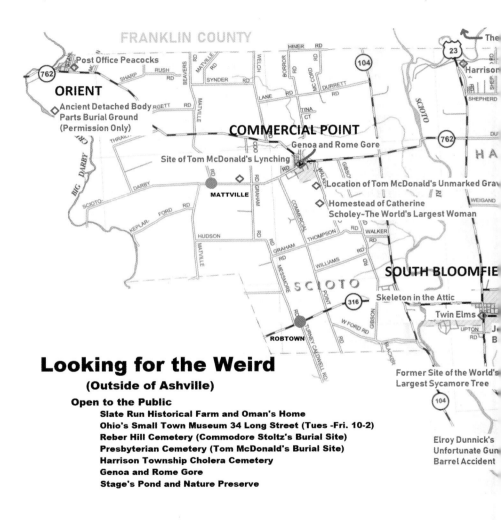

Looking for the Weird
(Outside of Ashville)

Open to the Public
- Slate Run Historical Farm and Oman's Home
- Ohio's Small Town Museum 34 Long Street (Tues -Fri. 10-2)
- Reber Hill Cemetery (Commodore Stoltz's Burial Site)
- Presbyterian Cemetery (Tom McDonald's Burial Site)
- Harrison Township Cholera Cemetery
- Genoa and Rome Gore
- Stage's Pond and Nature Preserve

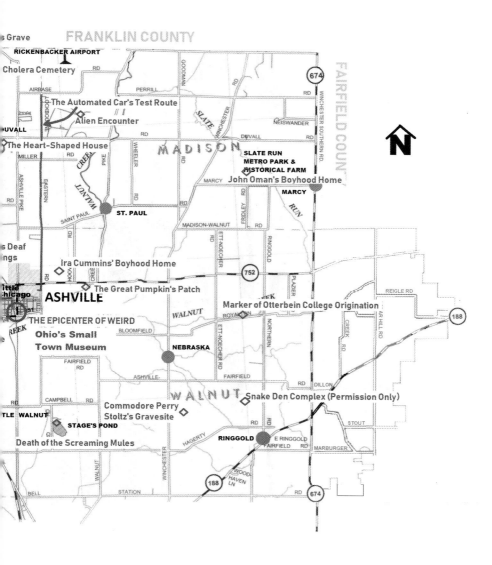

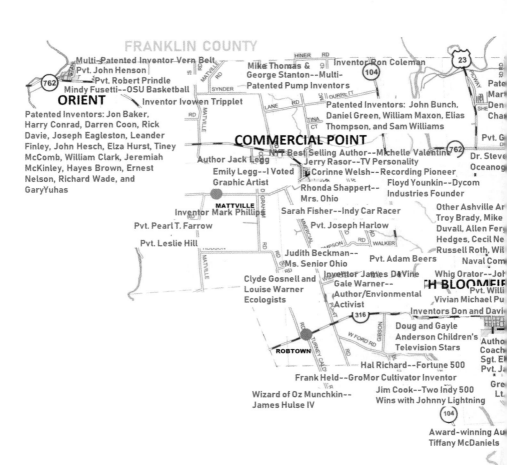

FRANKLIN COUNTY

Multi-Patented Inventor Vern Belt
Pvt. John Henson
Pvt. Robert Prindle
Mindy Fusetti--OSU Basketball
ORIENT
Inventor Ivowen Tripplet

Patented Inventors: Jon Baker,
Harry Conrad, Darren Coon, Rick
Davie, Joseph Eagleston, Leander
Finley, John Hesch, Elza Hurst, Tiney
McComb, William Clark, Jeremiah
McKinley, Hayes Brown, Ernest
Nelson, Richard Wade, and
GaryYuhas

Mike Thomas &
George Stanton--Multi-
Patented Pump Inventors

Inventor Ron Coleman

Patented Inventors: John Bunch,
Daniel Green, William Maxon, Elias
Thompson, and Sam Williams

COMMERCIAL POINT
NYT Best Selling Author--Michelle Valentine
Author Jack Legg
Jerry Rasor--TV Personality
Emily Legg--I Voted
Graphic Artist
Corinne Welsh--Recording Pioneer
Rhonda Shappert--
Mrs. Ohio
Floyd Younkin--Dycom
Industries Founder

MATTVILLE
Inventor Mark Phillips
Sarah Fisher--Indy Car Racer

Pvt. Pearl T. Farrow
Pvt. Joseph Harlow

Pvt. Leslie Hill
Judith Beckman--
Ms. Senior Ohio
Pvt. Adam Beers

Clyde Gosnell and
Louise Warner
Ecologists
Inventor James DeVine
Gale Warner--
Author/Envionmental
Activist

Doug and Gayle
Anderson Children's
ROBTOWN
Television Stars

Hal Richard--Fortune 500
Frank Held--GroMor Cultivator Inventor
Wizard of Oz Munchkin--
James Hulse IV
Jim Cook--Two Indy 500
Wins with Johnny Lightning

Dr. Steve
Oceanog

Other Ashville Ar
Troy Brady, Mike
Duvall, Allen Fer
Hedges, Cecil Ne
Russell Roth, Wil
Naval Com

Whig Orator--Joh
Pvt. Willi
Vivian Michael Pu
Inventors Don and Davi

Award-winning Au
Tiffany McDaniels

Looking for Wonderful Achievements
and Connections to History

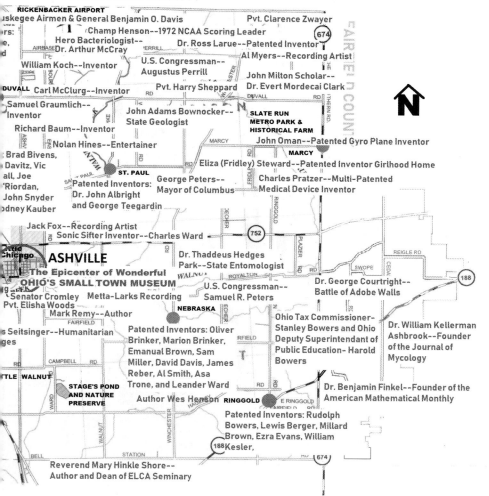

FRANKLIN COUNTY

RICKENBACKER AIRPORT
uskegee Airmen & General Benjamin O. Davis
rs:
e,
d
AIRBASE Dr. Arthur McCray
Champ Henson--1972 NCAA Scoring Leader
Hero Bacteriologist--
Dr. Ross Larue--Patented Inventor
Al Myers--Recording Artist
Pvt. Clarence Zwayer
674
William Koch--Inventor
U.S. Congressman--
Augustus Perrill
John Milton Scholar--
DUVALL Carl McClurg--Inventor
Pvt. Harry Sheppard
Dr. Evert Mordecai Clark
DUVALL
Samuel Graumlich--
Inventor
John Adams Bownocker--
State Geologist
SLATE RUN
METRO PARK &
HISTORICAL FARM
Richard Baum--Inventor
Nolan Hines--Entertainer
John Oman--Patented Gyro Plane Inventor
MARCY
Brad Bivens,
Davitz, Vic
all, Joe
Riordan,
John Snyder
dney Kauber
ST. PAUL
Patented Inventors:
Dr. John Albright
and George Teegardin
George Peters--
Mayor of Columbus
Eliza (Fridley) Steward--Patented Inventor Girlhood Home
Charles Pratzer--Multi-Patented
Medical Device Inventor
Jack Fox--Recording Artist
Sonic Sifter Inventor--Charles Ward
752
 hicago
ASHVILLE
The Epicenter of Wonderful
OHIO'S SMALL TOWN MUSEUM
Dr. Thaddeus Hedges
Park--State Entomologist
WALNUT ROYALTON
REIGLE RD
SWOPE
Dr. George Courtright--
Battle of Adobe Walls
188
Senator Cromley Metta-Larks Recording
Pvt. Elisha Woods
U.S. Congressman--
Samuel R. Peters
NEBRASKA
Mark Remy--Author
Seitsinger--Humanitarian
ges
Patented Inventors: Oliver
Brinker, Marion Brinker,
Emanual Brown, Sam
Miller, David Davis, James
Reber, Al Smith, Asa
Trone, and Leander Ward
Ohio Tax Commissioner-
Stanley Bowers and Ohio
Deputy Superintendant of
Public Education- Harold
Bowers
Dr. William Kellerman
Ashbrook--Founder
of the Journal of
Mycology
TLE WALNUT
STAGE'S POND
AND NATURE
PRESERVE
Author Wes Henson RINGGOLD
Dr. Benjamin Finkel--Founder of the
American Mathematical Monthly
Patented Inventors: Rudolph
Bowers, Lewis Berger, Millard
Brown, Ezra Evans, William
188 Kesler,
Reverend Mary Hinkle Shore--
Author and Dean of ELCA Seminary
674

Index